CHRISTIAN PROFICIENCY

also available from Cowley

English Spirituality
Spiritual Direction
A Joyful Heart
Prayer: A New Encounter

CHRISTIAN PROFICIENCY

MARTIN THORNTON

COWLEY PUBLICATIONS
CAMBRIDGE, MASSACHUSETTS

Published in the United States of America
by Cowley Publications.
International Standard Book No.: 0-936384-62-X.

Cover design by Monica Thornton.

First published in the United States in 1959 by Morehouse-Gorham Co.

COWLEY PUBLICATIONS
980 MEMORIAL DRIVE
CAMBRIDGE, MA 02138

To Alan Hockley

FOREWORD

A couple of years ago I was in Chicago, talking with a group of clergy before beginning a retreat with them, and I asked a question that I have asked frequently over the years: "What books would you like to see Cowley Publications bring out?" Without any hesitation one of the priests in the group said, "Martin Thornton's *Christian Proficiency.*" There it was again. How often that book came up whenever I asked that question. Maybe, I thought to myself, I had better find out for myself.

Sometime later, as I was browsing through our community library, I picked up a copy from the shelf. Just holding the book in my hands flooded me with memories. I remembered the kind, wise Christian Education professor, Dora Chaplin, who first recommended the book to me when I was a student at General Theological Seminary. She was a friend of Martin Thornton's and someone passionately concerned with the prayer lives of the students she was training for the ministry. And I remember what it was like to be a seminarian in my early twenties, wanting—but so uncertain about what it was to have—a life of prayer. Then I remembered what it was this book had given me that no other book on prayer had—practical sound service on how an ordinary person like me could pray. I remembered feeling relieved, hopeful, and grateful for this book. Perhaps, I said to myself, I could pray after all.

What is it like to read *Christian Proficiency* almost twenty years later? As someone who regularly listens to people talk about their struggles with prayer, I see more than ever the value of this book for lay people and clergy alike. Thornton reminds his readers what is central to the Anglican experience of prayer: the Eucharist, the daily office, and personal prayer. He gives commonsense advice about a rule of life, about the sacrament of penance, about what we can reasonably expect from personal prayer, and about retreats. Thornton answers those very questions many of us are too embarassed to ask.

Yet this is not a book for people who simply like to talk about prayer, or read about it, or think about it on the occasional walk through the woods or when gazing at a particularly stunning sunset. It is a book for people who want to do prayer—because they sense that prayer is crucial to the gift of baptism and their life in Christ, in his Body, the church. How important a book like this is, even thirty years after its first publication. How much balance it offers to the current fascination with self, the over-emphasis on personal prayer and feeling, which seem prevalent in the spirituality of today.

Christian Proficiency is also an amazingly warm, inviting, and pastoral approach to the life of prayer. Thornton knows ordinary people like us very well. He knows how frequently we are afraid to be honest with God in prayer. He knows how often we avoid real engagement with God in prayer, saying instead what we think Jesus would say, or what we think God wants to hear from us. Thornton shatters many of our most cherished illusions about prayer. He shows us how God is not much interested in what we would *like* to be, but how deeply God cares for us as we are, in all our humanity. The book is so clear and so unerringly accurate in its assessment of human nature that it will make you laugh out loud.

Martin Thornton was writing *Christian Proficiency* at about the same time I was growing up in the church in a small town in the midwest. So in some ways it will seem dated now. No doubt, being the keen pastor he was, Thornton would have wanted to revise it. For the book was written before liturgical renewal, before the ordination of women to the priesthood, before the church's plunge into many of the confusing and ambiguous issues of our comtemporary life. And yet I am quite happy to read the book as it is—not because it makes me nostalgic for the church I grew up in, but because it makes me wonder, in spite of our current concern for the laity, whether in some sense we have missed the boat. For Thornton takes the lay person very seriously. He takes the lay person just as he or she is, with the commitments of families and careers, without a great deal of theological education, without time for a lot of ministry or programs or more reading, and says, now this is how you can pray.

About the time that I was sitting down to write this foreword, I went to see the film *Babette's Feast*, the screen adaptation of a short story by Isak Dinesen. Set in a remote Danish village in the nineteenth century, it is the story of a famous Parisian chef who has endured fifteen years of serving plain austere dinners to a religious sect. Then she wins the lottery and decides to spend all the money on one enormous banquet for her benefactors. At the end of the movie the faithful, somewhat quarrelsome remnant of the stern, plain evangelical community sit down to eat Babette's luscious French cooking. It is a coming together of the flesh and the spirit, and it is a moment full of grace: the old folks begin to soften, and to smile, forgiving one another. Babette's elaborate, very sensual food becomes a eucharistic feast.

Martin Thornton's understanding of the Christian life of prayer and witness would heartily embrace such a feast, so close is it to his way of looking at God and at men and women in the life of prayer.

M. Thomas Shaw, SSJE
Cambridge, Massachusetts

CONTENTS

Cowley Publications is a work of the Society of St. John the Evangelist, a religious community for men in the Episcopal Church. The books we publish are a significant part of our ministry along with the work of preaching, spiritual direction, and hospitality.

1

"PROFICIENCY" IN CHRISTIAN TRADITION

> **Some . . . feeling any interior joy . . . abandon themselves to a sort of intoxication. . . . They fancy this is a trance and call it one, but I call it nonsense, it does nothing but waste their time. . . .**
>
> **ST TERESA**

THE TITLE of this book may sound curious to modern ears. Christianity is religion, and religion, to many, may be comforting, worrying, or mildly good for you. Its doctrine may be true or false, its prayer may be miraculously "answered", vaguely helpful, or just ignored, and its worship edifying, bewildering, stimulating, or dull. But the word "proficient" or "efficient" applies only to practical things like industry, agriculture, the army, or professional sport. This judgement is quite contrary to tradition; in fact these four things have all played considerable parts as analogies to the Christian life. St Benedict called the seven-fold Office "the work of God", the Cistercians were as efficient as farmers as they were as monks, the writings of St Ignatius Loyola teem with military terms, and "ascetic"—the technique and doctrine of prayer—comes from a Greek word meaning athletic training.

The life of Christ himself has been subjected to a nauseous sentimentality. None would deny his real humanity, his pastoral love and warm compassion, his feeling for Magdalene and his tears for Lazarus; but these mean nothing without the stern, disciplined duty which led to Gethsemane, the Passion and the Cross: this was his *work*. He not only loved his first disciples but trained them, and there is no reason to suppose that his attitude has altered. It is as well to remember that the word "disciple" is of the same root as the word "discipline".

The Sermon on the Mount, if you really look at it, is a most factual and dogmatic discourse, nearer to a technical lecture than a moral homily. The Eucharist, upon which the very existence of the Church depends, was instituted without fervour or explanation; "do this . . ." might well precede the sergeant-major's order to a new recruit. And of considerable significance to our present task was his reply to the Apostles' request "teach us to pray". As we shall soon see, the Lord's Prayer, given straight and without fuss, is the basis of what we now call ascetical theology. It is not only the most sublime of all prayers, it is also the most efficient plan of the whole art. It is not only pregnant with consolation, but with the whole structure of—to descend to a tautology the modern world nevertheless seems to need—"disciplined discipleship".

We need only mention the hard, practical, down-to-earth efficiency that underlies monastic Rule. Every minute of the day carefully laid out, prayer, worship, and work planned to the tiniest detail, minute rules for almsgiving and hospitality, not to mention rigorous penalties inflicted for the slightest deviation; this is no school of "sweet devotion".

But we must not exaggerate. If the pendulum has swung too far in one direction we gain little by swinging it too far in the other. Devotion to Our Lord, even "sensible" devotion, is a worthy thing, and all the great schools of Christian spirituality have produced it. But herein lie two dangers. First, the word "devotion" is liable to misinterpretation; it can be confused with mere emotion or a sentimental quest for nice feelings, whereas real devotion, like real faith, has its roots in volition. In fact discipline and devotion are not disparate for the one springs from the other, and that is the second point; we are in danger of seeking devotion without discipline, which is rather like trying to put the roof on a house before we have dug the foundations. The "devotional" section of the average bookshop usually contains little books of meditations and prayers and some of the great spiritual classics, but even these are of little use without a firm and efficient grounding in the practical life of prayer. It is only because of the blunt efficiency of the Cistercian discipline that a St Bernard could produce sublime works of devotion. St Thérèse of Lisieux, held by some to be the very epitome of sentimentality, and who called her *Life* "The springtime story of the Little White Flower", lived a life of rigour against which Commando training looks pretty mild.

Throughout the Christian tradition these two strands are interwoven; we have works of devotion and works of ascetic. The one is the fruit of the other because although devotion may incite us to prayer, only ascetic can tell us how to do it. In Christianity fact precedes feeling; what we do depends on what we are, and Pastoral Theology, by its very nature, is ever in danger of getting things the wrong way round. This is an important and very practical distinction about which the Proficient layman must be quite clear; he must realize, for example, that a book called "The Love of God" might be a devotional study of Our Lord's relation with John the beloved disciple, or it might be a philosophical treatise on the power by which all things were created and subsist. "Meditation" by Fr Brown might be the fruits of Fr Brown's private devotion, or it might be his ascetical instruction on how to make meditations; it might be devotional or it might be ascetic. As in the Church's tradition, so in the individual soul, there is need for both strands carefully balanced, but I will try to be more practical about this in Chapter 9. My one point here is that the idea of efficiency is no new thing, it is prior to, and the creator of, devotion in the true sense, and the Proficient must know what he is doing, what he is reading, and why.

There can be no doubt in which general direction the modern pendulum inclines. It is curious that the man who sticks to his job in illness, the sportsman who carries on in pain, the soldier who remains at his post in spite of wounds, are all subjects of admiration. None are doing brilliantly well but they are showing courage and stamina; we admire them in their hardship cheerfully borne, in their sinking of self-interest for the common good. Yet if we continue with our prayer when it is dull and arid, we are "insincere". If we assist at worship when we are ill, tired, and distracted, we are "irreverent", and when a man under intense temptation struggles, falls, confesses; struggles, falls, confesses, over and over again without despair, then he is a "hypocrite". Quite independent of interest or enthusiasm, work can be done efficiently, and prayer is work, vocation is the call to a job, conversion and Baptism imply not so much psychological experience as professional status.

We must re-learn the essential truth that Christian Prayer is rather like cleaning a car. When we are lucky enough to have a new one we wash and polish away with enthusiastic fervour, it is a devotional job. When the novelty wears off it becomes rather a nuisance and rather a bore, but we can still clean it efficiently, and here is the one vital point; there is no difference whatever in the result. It is exactly the same with prayer, and in the next chapter I will try to explain why.

2

"PROFICIENCY" AND DOCTRINE

Clearly we must work hard.

ST TERESA

I HAVE promised not to burden the ordinary Christian with a lot of complicated theology for its own sake. But it is only reasonable, in the cause of efficiency itself, to know why we do certain things as well as knowing how to do them. Offices, sacraments, and prayers may be compared with work in a factory; the end product of world redemption really flows from the work of a team of efficient workmen in the Church. But if work consists of fitting one particular nut to one particular bolt, all day long, it is no bad thing to learn a little about the total process; we might as well know whether we are making a sewing machine or an aeroplane. If a good deal of our Christian work consists of saying the same old psalms over and over again we might as well understand how it all fits in with the total process.

Christianity has been called the most materialistic of all religions. I would prefer to call it the most efficient. I do not simply mean that it is better, higher, or nearer the truth—though indeed it is all this—but that its unique doctrines point to, and finally demand, this kind of approach. And the doctrines which most concern us here are the very basis of our faith, prayer, and life: the Holy Trinity, the Incarnation, and the Church. We are concerned with what are known as the "Three Heavenly Unities"—the unity of the three Persons in the Godhead, the unity of God and Man in Christ, and the unity of Christ and the Church.

I

The doctrine of the Trinity, far from being merely academic, is the expression of the most fundamental human experience, and, we shall see later, it is of much practical use. Only the view that God is transcendent, majestic, almighty, the creator of the universe and standing outside it, can fully satisfy the human mind. Yet we know that he must also be immanent, in the world, close to us, giving us life; "in him we live, and move, and have our being". And this is an absurd contradiction without the mediation of the second Person of the Trinity. This experience is common to all men, though only the Christian revelation adequately expresses it, that is why the idea is hinted at, groped after, throughout the Old Testament: Jehovah the God of all, the Messiah, his anointed, and the indwelling Wisdom.

Without this conception of God as Unity-in-Trinity, which itself sets Christianity apart from any other system, religion must tend towards one of two things. Either it is immanental and worldly,[1] like Confucianism, which becomes very largely ethical. It fails to face the fact—never mind the theory—of original sin and experience proves that however laudable it may be to proclaim the brotherhood of nations and to exhort men to love one another, it has singularly little effect; it just does not work. And it must be admitted that the type of so-called Christianity that puts all the emphasis on the moral teaching of Jesus is not likely to fare much better. Or non-trinitarian religion is transcendental, or other-worldly,[1] to the point of complete world renunciation, like a good deal of Eastern religion. This faces the fact of present evil but the only hope is to escape from it altogether and become "absorbed" in God. Not unnaturally, such religion reaches great heights of a certain type of mystical and contemplative prayer. The one tries to influence the world for good and fails, the other is not interested in the world at all: neither is very efficient.

Christianity certainly faces the fact of sin and evil, but it realizes that the fallen world can only be restored by God, it can only be "picked up" by a power outside itself; "you

[1] But see Chapter 14.

cannot", says Dr Mascall, "raise yourself off the floor by tightening your braces". But if Christianity will have nothing to do with the idea of the human world's self-improvement, neither does it teach its total depravity: it speaks of *redemption.*

II

Redemption is won by the triumph of Christ on the Cross. That is the central, practical fact that the most "ordinary" Christian accepts, there is no need here to go especially deep into the doctrine of the Atonement—although it is wise to think and meditate about it another time (see Chapter 7, IV). What we must do is to consider one or two points about the Incarnation itself, upon which it all depends. As briefly as possible, Jesus Christ is perfectly God and perfectly man; because he is God he has the power of redemption, because he is man he is in a position to use it. Now when we say that Christ is man, we mean two interrelated things; he is truly and perfectly a *man* "like unto us in all things, sin except" but he is also a new humanity, summing up the whole human race in himself. In Dr Mascall's words:

"There is thus in Christ a new creation of manhood out of the material of the fallen human race. There is continuity with the fallen race through the manhood taken from Mary; there is discontinuity through the fact that the Person of Christ is the pre-existent Logos." (Word, Son of God, eternal second person of the Trinity.) "In Christ human nature has been re-created by the very God who was its first creator; and the new creation is effected, not like the first creation by the mere decree of omnipotent will—'Let us make man in our own image'—but by the creator himself becoming man and moulding human nature to the lineaments of his own Person. Christ is thus quite literally the Second Adam, the man in whom the human race begins anew; but while the first Adam was, in all his innocence, only God's creature, the Second Adam is the Creator himself. In him human nature is made afresh, and in him the mysterious distortion which succeeding generations have inherited from man's first disobedience, and which theology knows as original sin, has no place."[1]

[1] *Christ, the Christian and the Church*, p. 3.

The tremendous fact is that our fallen human nature can be redeemed, or renewed, or regenerated, by this new manhood of Christ; we can really share in the new humanity of Christ and, of special importance here, we can really share in his redemptive work. This new *humanity* of Christ is a permanent thing, it is not simply the human nature of Christ which he "had" during his life on earth, but the new all-embracing humanity now risen, ascended, and glorified, unrestricted by time and space, in which we can truly share. When we speak about "putting off the old Adam and putting on the new Man" we are not talking of possible moral effort but of a certain acquired status. Dr Mascall sums it up thus:

"It is almost universally assumed to-day that becoming a Christian means in essence the adoption of a new set of beliefs or the initiation of a new mode of behaviour. A Christian would be defined as one who 'believes in Christ' or 'worships Christ' or 'tries to follow Christ's teaching'. Now it is far from my purpose to belittle either Christian dogma or Christian ethics. Nevertheless, it must be pointed out that to define the essence of Christianity in terms either of belief or of practice involves the neglect of two principles that are fundamental to all sound theology. The former of these is that the act of God precedes and is presupposed by the acts of man: 'Herein is love, not that we loved God, but that he loved us';[1] 'Ye have come to know God, *or rather to be known of God.*'[2] The second is that what a being *is* precedes what it *does*; our actions are a consequence of what we are. . . . It will follow from this that the Christian should be defined not in terms of what he himself does, but of what God has made him to be. Being a Christian is an ontological fact, resulting from an act of God.

"What, then, is this act by which God makes a man into a Christian? It is, the New Testament assures us, incorporation into the human nature of Christ, an incorporation by which the very life of the Man Christ Jesus is communicated to us and we are re-created in him. 'I am the vine; ye are the branches'; 'If any man is in Christ, he is a new creature', or 'there is a new creation'; we have been 'grafted into' Christ

[1] 1 John 4.10. [2] Gal. 4.9.

like shoots into a tree.[1] The Christian is a man to whom something has *happened*, something moreover which is irreversible and which penetrates to the very roots of his being; he is a man who has been re-created in, and into, Christ.

"Now the basis of this ontological change by which a man becomes a Christian is the permanence of the human nature of Christ. We have already seen . . . how necessary it is to hold that the divine Word really became flesh, that he united to himself, unconfusedly and inseparably, a concrete human nature, and that that human nature, though glorified by his Resurrection and Ascension and no longer subject to the limitations which governed it during the period of his humiliation, is nevertheless still in existence and still fully human.[2] As the Epistle to the Hebrews teaches, it is with his manhood still intact and for ever united to his divine Person that Christ has entered into the realm of the 'heavenlies', there to make perpetual intercession for us. The re-creation of manhood in Christ was not finished when, in the womb of Mary, he had united a perfect and unblemished human nature to himself, or even when in that human nature, by his death on Calvary, he had, as our representative, offered to the Father the oblation of love and obedience that we were powerless to offer ourselves. The truth is not merely that in Christ the new creation was effected on our behalf, but that through our union with him it is to be brought about in each one of us. Becoming a Christian means being re-created by being incorporated into the glorified manhood of the ascended Christ, so that, in the words of the Epistle to the Ephesians, we are raised up with him and made to sit with him in the heavenly places, in Jesus Christ.[3]

"Now the normal and divinely appointed means by which this re-creation is initiated is clearly the Sacrament of Baptism, the sacrament of new birth, of regeneration."[4]

This passage is well worth a little effort, for once we understand it we see that, contrary to so much sentiment and misunderstanding, "conversion" is simply an invitation to Baptism; not just joining in fellowship with like-minded

[1] John 15.2; Cor. 5.17; Rom. 11.13–24. [2] See p. 30 *supra*.
[3] Eph. 2.16. [4] *Christ, the Christian and the Church*, pp. 77–8.

people who believe certain things and behave in a certain way, but acquiring a new, eternal, supernatural status. Incorporation into the humanity of the Redeemer means actively sharing the work of redemption. In practice, being a Christian means accepting both a job and the tools with which to do it, and a Christian can be plainly, fully, and accurately defined as "one who has been Baptized". The baptized soul can "lose his faith", refuse the sacraments, give up prayer, and constantly commit the most scandalous sins; which would make him a very bad and inefficient Christian, but a Christian nevertheless. Baptism remains the irrevocable act of God which "has happened to him" as surely as he has been born of particular parents in a particular place: extreme excitability, a loathing for cricket, and a passion for garlic may be a little odd in a Yorkshireman, but they do not turn him into an Italian.

Quite apart from the significance of this theology, it is precisely the kind of knowledge that is needed for the minor but still important function of evangelism and apologetic in daily life. How often is the acknowledged Christian assailed in factory, office, and pub with: "Christians are no better than anybody else"; or "Look at this terrible scandal about So-and-So—and he pretended to be a Christian, what has the Church done for him? Surely he will never go again." Silly questions no doubt, but they might as well receive the right answers, we might as well have strong apologetic rather than weak apology. In fact, Christians may or may not be better than others, but they are certainly different creatures from the unbaptized, with different supernatural powers and with the tools of the trade of world redemption. In fact poor old So-and-So, painful as his lapse may be, *is* a Christian by Baptism and no amount of scandal can alter the fact, he has never "pretended" to be other than what Baptism has made him, the Church has done a great deal for him and, by confession, penance, and absolution, can do a great deal more; and he must certainly "go to Church" more than ever before. And, of course, "Why are you a Christian anyway?" Even the most faithful and loyal members of Christ's Body find themselves embarrassed and frustrated by attacks of this sort, and I suggest that, apart from the particular doctrine concerned, the general weakness is that our Faith is interpreted in terms of "devotion", conviction and feeling instead of efficiency and fact. But that is something of a diversion.

The Proficient Christian is far more than a good man who helps others and sets a high moral example—and it is not impossible for him to be reasonably efficient without doing either; he is essentially a Member of Christ. And here "member" is used in the sense of the "limb" of a Body, not merely as we speak of a member of a club or college; these may indeed boast some sort of corporate bond but they do not form a living organism in the strict sense. Now it is obvious that the efficiency of bodily limbs depends entirely on the efficiency of the whole bodily organism; and "ye are the Body of Christ and severally members thereof".[1]

III

We come now to the third of the Heavenly Unities, and return to Dr Mascall:

"Becoming a Christian, as we have seen, means being incorporated into the human nature of Christ, the very human nature which he united to his divine Person in the womb of the Blessed Virgin and which he offered upon the Cross as 'a full, perfect and sufficient sacrifice, oblation and satisfaction for the sins of the whole world', the human nature which in his Resurrection and Ascension has been glorified and set free from the spatial limitations of ordinary human existence. This adoptive union with the triumphant Christ is altogether unique in its kind; it involves a real participation in Christ's human nature on the part of the believer and a real communication of it to him. By it the believer's own human nature is not destroyed but is strengthened and perfected by its grafting into the archetypal human nature of the Ascended Lord. There is no destruction of the created person, nor in being supernaturalized is he removed from the natural order. His life as a citizen of Earth continues, but he has a new and

[1] 1 Cor. 12.27.

greater citizenship in Heaven. He is a new man, because he has been re-created in the New Adam. And because the Christ is both God and man, the Christian, by his incorporation into Christ, has received a share in the life of God himself. He has been made a partaker of the divine nature, the nature of God who is Trinity. His life is hid with Christ in God.

"It is this fact of incorporation and adoption that is the ontological basis of the Christian Church."[1]

It is also the basis of St Paul's great doctrine of the Church as the "Body of Christ", but before we look at its practical implications, let us indulge in another little diversion into everyday apologetics. In the passage above it will be seen that by Baptism the soul is raised to a supernatural level of Spirit and Grace; on which he literally shares in the redeeming life of Christ. Plainly the part he is called upon to play in the process of world redemption is only possible by activity on this level. The most direct and truly practical way we can serve the world is by prayer and by sacramental acts; only Grace redeems nature and God's acts precede those of men. But on the other hand the Christian has not lost his own human nature, and he is still called upon to exert his God-given strength in solving the social and moral problems of his day and age. He is still an agent of free will; the Heavenly citizen is still concerned with London, Leeds, and Manchester. Thus a "Christian" and a "Churchman" are exact synonyms, because the Church is Christ's Body into which we are grafted. The Church exists before her members because God comes before men. The Church is eternal because Christ is eternal. So to return to the pub: "Can you be a Christian without going to Church?" Without going to Church to be baptized, categorically "No". The baptized soul who does not "go to Church" is irrevocably a Christian, and always will be, but without the Sacraments of Grace he is living a lie, he is living outside the truth of his own being, he is in fact the complete "hypocrite"—far more so than all the wicked people who go to Mass and Confession. Moreover, however many social welfare committees he serves, however many hospitals and homes he endows, he remains a moral ostrich;

[1] *Christ, the Christian and the Church*, p. 109.

in face of sin and suffering he is burying his head in the sand because he avoids the one and only channel of redemption. Then there is the man who prefers the radio service to his parish church, which may indeed be more edifying; but Our Lord seems to have omitted to tell us on which wave-length sacramental Grace is purveyed.

Again: "Christianity is losing ground, the churches are empty, it is outdated, soon the Church will be superseded by communism or socialism or humanism or some other -ism." But the Church is the Body of the Eternal Christ, in Heaven, Paradise, and on earth, she is antecedent to her worldly members. Every Christian in the world could be slaughtered tomorrow, every church, chapel, and cathedral razed to the ground, every Bible and prayer-book, every word of Christian theology and devotion, could be destroyed; and it would not make the slightest difference to the existence of the "Church". On the surface "the Church cannot survive" sounds a reasonable prophecy, "the glorified humanity of Christ cannot survive" sounds ridiculous; yet both statements mean exactly the same thing. Every living Christian could apostatize today, and it would make not the remotest bit of difference to Christian "Truth". Of course a great many people will not believe this—which makes little difference either—but it is still the right answer. Needless to say until these tragedies happen, we must get on with the job.[1]

"We must therefore take quite seriously the Pauline terminology in which the Church is described as the Body of Christ. This does not, of course, mean that we can find in the Church an exact duplication of the various organs of a physical body; the efforts of some Roman-Catholic writers to particularize the Church's heart and neck seem to be somewhat strained, and to extend the identification to other organs would become rapidly ludicrous and irreverent."[2]

While taking this warning seriously to heart, I still think we might extend the analogy just a little further for purposes of pastoral illustration. I think for example that there is a real truth behind the common devotional metaphor of the

[1] *Christ, the Christian and the Church*, see Chapter 7, sec. 3, p. 118.
[2] Ibid., p. 110.

Eucharist as the soul's "spiritual food". In one sense—though this statement contains dangers—the Lord's Last Supper is his Mystical Body's first meal. And after all, St Paul himself went so far as to speak of eyes, ears, and noses in this connection.[1] So, for illustration, the Body of Christ, like a human body, lives and works by food and exercise; by the Eucharist and by the spiritual exercise of prayer. If the Christian comes into being by the baptismal re-birth, lives by food and exercise, he may well need the occasional operations of Penance and Holy Unction by a "Physician of the soul". From this, two significant facts emerge—indeed they form the basis of this book: the first is that if we remember the root meaning of the word "ascetic" it becomes clear that the food, exercise, medicine, and work of the Body—interpreted either universally or locally[2]—is a matter of system and order. Our food must be balanced and our exercise must be disciplined. The second point is that the efficiency of the work of its members, its hands and legs, eyes and lips—again interpreted either universally or locally—depends entirely upon the general health of the whole Body. The redemptive channel of Grace flowing from Christ on to the world—or town or parish—is not the individual Christian but the Church. Really effective prayer is that, not so much of the contemplative saint and the "sincerely devout" Christian, but the total prayer of the integral Body. Two further very practical and very modern pastoral points follow: all the prayer we offer, every act of corporate worship and every "private" prayer, is but a part of the total prayer of the Church; neither the mystical heights of the contemplative saint nor the routine office of the dullest Proficient have any great value in their own right. Yet both have supreme value in that they add to the prayer of the Church; they are inter-dependent, the latter shares in the former, which in turn, depends on its support. The effective prayer of the Body of Christ itself implies "balance" between "devotion" and routine; there can be not the slightest doubt on which side the modern need lies. "The effectual fervent prayer of a righteous man availeth much."[3] But the routine

[1] 1 Cor. 12.15–24. [2] See my *Pastoral Theology*, Chapter 4.
[2] James 5.16

prayer of the Church availeth a good deal more –and St James would be the last to deny it. And from the practical worldly angle "in the Mystical Body, life and worship are but two elements in one great act, the self-offering of Christ the God-Man to the Father in heaven. Life itself is liturgical."[1] Works of charity by Christians are linked with, are indeed part of, the total prayer of the Church: again there can be no argument as to which side needs the extra weight. Without offence, a good many of our parishes are rather like a sentimental weight-lifter with a weak heart.

It follows that the very ordinary Proficient member of the very ordinary parish, need have no heartsearchings as to his value, he need never bemoan his lack of gifts, or despair at the constancy of his temptations: humility yes, but he need never feel that he is not pulling his weight or think himself useless to others. The lone fighter-pilot may get the medals—and rightly—but without a large, efficient, trained ground-crew, he would not get into the air at all: the expression "mystical flights" is here most apposite.

The channel of redemption is the Mystical Body itself, and its power is Prayer in its widest and deepest sense, which is, to St Thomas Aquinas: "Loving God in act so that the divine Love may communicate itself to us, and through us to the world."

As one would expect from this source, "Love" is both the devotional bond which attracts us to Christ, that which is manifested by his life and death, and also the creative and redemptive power of God by which all things exist. Again as one would expect, "us" is a kind of corporate plural, not an aggregate of Christians (which would be meaningless to St Thomas) but the one organic Body. So the Church Militant, one with the triumphant Church in Heaven, is the channel, the Body, the organism, almost the "machinery", through which the redemptive Grace flows from Christ himself on to the world around it. It is vicarious.

"Since the very essence of the Church is the human nature of Christ communicated to men by adoption and incorporation, it follows that the sole channel of grace to the world is the

[1] *Christian, the Christian and the Church*, p. 164.

Church. Christ and his Bride are one flesh."[1] But "we can hold with perfect firmness to the doctrine that salvation and grace are mediated only through the Church and still see their effects manifested throughout the human race, even in those who have never heard of Christ; we may indeed see the effects of the Incarnation in a gradual supernaturalization of the whole created order. For the Incarnation was not only something happening to Christ; it was something happening to the world itself, inasmuch as God the Word united to himself the nature of man, in whom the created order reaches its culmination and in whose praise and service towards God the purpose for which the world was created—the glory of God—reaches its rational and articulate expression."[2]

In pastoral terms, the normal healthy functioning of the Body, the cleansing of the channel, the oiling of the machinery if you like; the Mass, the Office, and the prayer of its members: this is the redemptive work of the Church, this is the supreme work in which we may delight, we may be consoled, we may be elated, but we *must* be efficient. And as we accept our share in the prayers of the mystics and the saints, so we may be assured of our part in all good works from whatever immediate source they come. "Clearly we must work hard."

[1] Ibid., p. 149. In Chapter 7, we must say a little about the ascetical implications of the Church seen as the Bride of Christ: here we might point out that although a bride is loving towards her husband, although she rightly hopes to beget children, there is still the cleaning, cooking, and washing up.

[2] Ibid., p. 150. *See also* p. 149, note 1.

3

THE CHRISTIAN FRAMEWORK

Let all things be done decently and in order.

ST PAUL

I AM tempted to call this chapter "The Skeleton" because it is to deal with the frame or supporting structure of the "Body", and I intend to disregard Dr Mascall's warning[1]—just this once—if only for illustration. So dare we think of the Eucharist as the living heart of the Body of Christ, of the Office as its continual beat, its pulse, and private prayer as the circulation of the blood giving life and strength to its several members according to their need and capacity? Of course this is illustration not theology, yet I think it gives a fair picture of the facts. At least it demonstrates the certainty that the prayer and life of each member is wholly dependent on the health of the total organism; private prayer is absolutely dependent on the Office and the Mass.

I

In more worthy terms, the health and growth of an individual's prayer life—its proficiency—depends on the truth of his conception of God, and the Christian God is One Holy and undivided Trinity, manifested to us in Jesus Christ. God is transcendent Father, indwelling Spirit, and Incarnate Word: One God.

"And in this Trinity none is afore, or after other: none is greater, or less than another;
But the whole three Persons are co-eternal together: and co-equal.
So that in all things, as is aforesaid: the Unity in Trinity, and the Trinity in Unity is to be worshipped."

[1] See p. 13.

In my *Pastoral Theology* I have tried to show, at considerable length and in much detail, how this theology finds practical expression in the Office objectively "given" to God Almighty, the Eucharist centred upon Our Lord Jesus Christ, and private prayer inspired by the Holy Ghost. And it follows that the three parts of this framework—Office, Mass, private prayer—are as indissociable one from another as the three Persons of the Trinity himself. There is no need to repeat these arguments.[1] I am concerned here with the ordinary Proficient Christian and his private prayer, but I am bound to insist, as strongly as I possibly can, that here and throughout the whole book I am treating private prayer as but one part of the whole integrated Christian life. It can never be a "separate" subject and as the previous chapter should have made clear, there is a sense in which there can be no such thing as "private" prayer, since *all* prayer is but part of the total prayer of the Church. What is meant here is that part of the prayer-life that the soul pursues *physically* alone, according to his own unique gifts, personality and temperament: however alone he may be physically or geographically, or however alone he may feel emotionally, he and his prayer remain in and of the Body of Christ. I am convinced that any book on private prayer wherein this trinitarian pattern is neglected or taken out of focus could do incalculable damage to Christian souls. I am not merely saying, "Here is a book about private prayer—but it is a good thing to join in corporate worship as well"; I am insisting that Mass-Office-private prayer forms one whole balanced organic *life*.

Because by incorporation into Christ we do not lose our unique personality, our prayer must be both the actual prayer *of* Christ to the Father, and our own personal prayer *to* Christ —or to the Father "through Jesus Christ our Lord". It is here that the doctrine of the Church as the Body of Christ needs to be supplemented by the analogy of the Bride of Christ, for although in marriage the "twain are one flesh" the twain can nevertheless talk to one another. We are "in Christ" by Baptism, and we continue to live in him and worship the Father in him, directly through the sacraments

[1] *Pastoral Theology: a Reorientation*, pp. 192–247.

and the Office, but we can also talk *to* him, individually, in private prayer: incorporation into Christ does not mean that in petition the Christian is talking to himself! And it follows that the sacraments of incorporation and life in Christ, and the regular offering of the total Body—Mass and Office—take precedence over personal private prayer however exalted. This contradicts nothing I have said in the last paragraph since it is but the pastoral counterpart to the fact that Christ is "Equal to the Father, as touching his Godhead: and inferior to the Father, as touching his manhood." So to be very practical, although all three parts must enter into the full Christian life, in the event of emergency Mass and Office come before formal private prayer. Of course this does not make private prayer unimportant, or strictly speaking less important, but before we finally settle down to consider it there is one further point about liturgical worship which might be useful.

Manuals and instructions on the liturgy are invariably couched in idealistic terms; they are mainly "devotional", and although it is good to have a clear ideal at which to aim, this is not very practical by itself. There is one little Mass book, ostensibly for children, which, at the elevation of the sacred Host, gives the curt direction "look up and adore"—excellent advice, no doubt, but it is rather like telling a golfer to hit the ball off the tee and into the hole: it is not quite so easy as it sounds. If it is not an irreverent comparison, both imply the very peak of perfection. We must go on striving for the ideal and around the throne of the Lamb in Heaven we may reach it, but meanwhile can we be proficient? I think we can; by distinguishing three very lowly yet not wholly ineffective stages in the "technique of going to Church".

First, despite distractions, sins, headaches, drowsiness, boredom, and aridity, we can just go; we can be there. And we can be there in good faith, by which I mean we can recognize that the Mass is primarily an act of God and not of man. It is the action of the whole Body of which we are members, and its influence is quite independent of the fervour or devotion of celebrant or laity, but it cannot be celebrated without both; we truly take part by just being there. If we are the sole lay representative we are performing the most important possible function—sins and feelings notwithstanding. I need hardly add that I am in no way advocating slovenly or ill-prepared participation in the Mass, nor am I saying that attention and devotion do not matter. I am saying that in bad and difficult times, we can throw everything upon the divine action of Christ, do our poor best, fail miserably, and stop worrying; "being there" is a lowly yet efficient act.

Second, without much devotion or fervour, we can follow the action of the Mass with a cold and probably undistracted recognition of what it is. We may fail to "look up and adore" but we shall recognize, by faith and by will, that Christ is there; we may not feel his Presence and we may forget the theology of it all. We may not be fervent but we are obedient.

Lastly, illumination, sensible devotion, spontaneous acts of praise and resolution, enter in to the mere recognition of stage two. Let there be no mistake that this is a real advance. And in the cause of Christian proficiency—not to mention theology—let there be no notion that any of these things make the remotest scrap of difference as to what the Mass *is* or what it *does*, or who does it.

The same kind of principle can be applied to the Office, although its technique and emphasis are quite different. But I have treated this elsewhere.[1]

If this three-fold Rule of the Church—Mass, Office, private prayer—is the basis of a single prayer-life, the expression of active faith in God the Holy Trinity, it follows that private prayer itself must be governed by pattern and design. If the Body is an organic whole, then, in a derivative sense, so is each member. The efficiency of the hand depends not only on the heartbeat but upon a complex harmony between knuckles, muscles, and joints; we all know how the slightest cut on the little finger makes the use of the whole hand clumsy and awkward. Yet so many writers, especially of the older Protestant school, treat private prayer as a list of items rather than a planned design. In a famous book by the German Lutheran, Friedrich Heiler, called simply *Prayer*, we find a most exhaustive and useful list of every conceivable type. But, as one

[1] *Pastoral Theology: a Reorientation*, pp. 205–17.

example, his much lauded "primitive prayer from the heart" is compared with the *mere* "recitation of formulae". The fact that I disagree with that valuation—though I think orthodoxy supports me—is beside the point. What is completely missed is the possibility that these two different types of prayer might still be complementary; that any number of prayer forms might create a system more creative than the mere sum of them all.

As with the overall Rule of the Church, private prayer is itself divisible into three main sections. First, mental prayer, in its widest sense, by which we increase our knowledge, love, and communion with God manifested in Christ. Second, Colloquy: simply "saying our prayers"—although the use of this rather technical word is necessary. This includes all the usual sub-divisions: Petition, intercession, thanksgiving, confession, etc. And thirdly, Recollection, which consists simply of momentary acts of prayer throughout the working day; a simple, periodic "practice of the Presence of God".

The complete Christian life of prayer can thus be set out as a regular pattern:

A	B	C
I. OFFICE		
II. MASS		
III. PRIVATE PRAYER:	1. Mental Prayer	
	2. Colloquy:	*a.* Petition
		b. Self-examination and Confession
		c. Intercession
		d. Thanksgiving—— (almsgiving)
		e. Adoration
	3. Recollection———	(fasting)

At first sight this, like most tables, looks much more complicated than it really is. A closer look will show that it contains little or nothing more than the most "ordinary" Christian is doing already; anyone aiming at proficiency goes to Mass, has some part in the Office—though this may be the weak point for many—and tries to say his prayers and live with God. The table, which is only the basic Rule of the Church, contains no more than that, and proficiency (or sanctity for that matter) depends not on doing *more* than the soul is probably doing already but on doing the same things in a design instead of in a muddle. It is a question of pattern and perspective, and especially of a pattern of prayer which makes for a Christian design in the whole of life.

II

If such a scheme still seems a little artificial or arbitrary, it can now be examined in the light of the best possible authority, as the simplest and most practical analysis of the Lord's Prayer. If it were argued that the Lord's Prayer was given us to be said and not analysed, I would be bound to disagree—though I do not mean that it should never be said! To give plain, direct orders, then leave the living experience of the Church to work out their details and gradually gain insight into their profound wisdom, is precisely Our Lord's method. The Church's Rule, as tabulated, is the fruit of just such experience. Thus:

Our Father which art in heaven, hallowed be thy Name: We have noticed two things about the word "Our". First, this is not simply the prayer Christ taught his disciples, it is also the prayer he still offers to the Father through the members of his Body. We are sons not servants only by incorporation into Christ, only the baptized can say "Our Father". It is the prayer of the Church exclusively; if those outside the Church say the Lord's Prayer, they are putting sentiment before fact, they are praying less than the truth if not blatant lies:

"It is in Christ alone that we can cry 'Abba, Father'. The Lord's Prayer, the *Pater Noster*, is the Church's prayer, the prayer of those who dare to approach God with the name 'Father' upon their lips only because the sonship they had forfeited has been restored to them in Christ."[1]

"Our" is also St Thomas' corporate plural; in the most private of "private" prayer it remains Our not My Father, the most "private" prayer is a part of the prayer of the Church. But a "formula" given to the Church (the school of Heiler please note!) suggests recital in common—the Office. Adoration is given first place in the pattern prayer, it is the

[1] *Christ, the Christian and the Church*, p. 95.

peak of spiritual achievement. In context, practically the whole Rule is contained in this clause alone.

Thy Kingdom come: "The kingdom of God is within you", by Baptismal incorporation into the Mystical Body, we are in it. The kingdom of God is the Church, its capital is the Heavenly City, but it was established on earth in the village of Bethlehem. The kingdom of God came down with the Incarnation, it comes down in every Eucharist.

Thy will be done in earth as in heaven: But life in Christ strengthens personality, it does not suppress it; we are *incorporated* not *absorbed* into Christ. So individuals are to strive to play their personal part in achieving the will of God in the world. Action springs from prayer, private action is qualified by "private" prayer, nature is only redeemed by Grace, and all is directed by the Holy Ghost. These first three clauses point to a unified life of prayer in the Holy Trinity; transcendence - mediation - immanence: Office - Mass - private prayer. And this last points to the unity of the three-fold Church; Triumphant-Expectant-Militant here on earth.

Give us this day our daily bread: The Church is not materialistic but sacramental, which is why bodies and things are so important. We all partake of the One Bread yet retain our individuality. This is petition.

And forgive us our trespasses as we forgive them that trespass against us: As we shall see very soon, confession flows out of real petition as surely as night follows day, in fact petition, self-examination, and confession are nearly the same thing. It all follows inevitably from knowing Christ better though mental prayer. The conditional phrase brings us back to worldly responsibility, both personal and corporate intertwined. Sacramental confession, in one way the most "private" of prayers, is of vicarious and corporate significance: it is part of the prayer of the Church.

And lead us not into temptation but deliver us from evil: A very "worldly" workmanlike petition, the outcome of universal experience. We are to seek the constant protection of God throughout every day of our lives; that is the habit of Recollection.

The concluding doxology completes the circle and brings

us back, through thanksgiving, to the corporate Adoration of God the most Holy and undivided Trinity.

This authoritative, orthodox framework for the Christian life of prayer, a simple, unified, and creative whole, implies two preliminaries at which I have more than hinted in this chapter. First, all my analogies—or rather the Church's analogies—show that prayer is, if not unduly difficult, then at least a "technical" thing. The very idea of Proficiency implies a serious yet common-sense approach to it. All souls are unique, all the ascetical theology there is would be insufficient to cover each and every individual difficulty or particular gift; and the ordinary Proficient Christian does not want to be bothered with more theology than is absolutely necessary. The straightforward answer is personal *Spiritual Direction.*

Secondly, I have said that creative prayer, proficient prayer, does not necessarily mean *more* prayer. It means pattern, design, shape, system, balance—words we are all getting rather tired of; and the proper term for this is *Rule*, a technical word from the Latin *Regula* associated especially with St Benedict.

Both these words, and the ideas behind them, are so hopelessly misunderstood, so frequently misinterpreted, and they are surrounded by so much prejudice; that I will try to explain their real meaning at once.

4

SPIRITUAL DIRECTION

If anyone makes himself his own master in the spiritual life, he makes himself scholar to a fool.

ST BERNARD

I

IT MAY BE just possible to learn music, algebra, chemistry, or golf by a mixture of text-books, public lectures, and private experiment, but there is no real substitute for personal tuition. Even in more commonplace things like housework, cooking, or gardening, we rely more than we realize on the advice of others: our parents or our friends. In very little are we really "self-taught"; the successful gardener who makes such a claim has probably spent the early years of his life asking his neighbour if it is time to plant cabbages, and consulting the fellow over the road about pruning roses. In its barest essence, spiritual direction is just so common an everyday principle applied to religious life. In prayer as in most other things the self-taught are not usually very proficient, except possibly in the case of genius and here we are not concerned with genius but "ordinary" Christians, and the more "ordinary" they are the more they need personal direction.

In some ways "Direction" and "Director" (who is usually but not necessarily a priest) are unfortunate words, but they are so firmly embedded in tradition that I think we must retain them. Words like "guide", "coach", "mentor" would be better and more acceptable today, but I think their use would only add different misconceptions. (In fact this has happened with the recent introduction of the term "counsellor" which we must notice a little later.) Suffice it to say here that we receive direction from a priest in the same sense as from a policeman; he advises us to follow a certain road to get to a certain place, he may give us a choice of routes and point out their respective snags and merits. He does not order us against our will—unless it is a one-way street when it is better to follow his direction all the same—nor does he get out his car and take us there himself. I must be content to deny, firmly and finally, that direction has anything whatever to do with autocracy, "priestcraft", submissiveness, easy ways out, not standing on one's own feet, interfering with the relation between the soul and God, etc., etc., etc. It is none of these things and the direct opposite of most of them.

But if learning music, golf, or gardening, or asking policemen the way, illustrate the basis of spiritual direction, none of these is sufficient to explain it fully. Direction has special values in its own right which may be generally grouped under five headings:

(1) Let it never be forgotten that the most private direction in the most private prayer is still concerned with the total prayer of the Body of Christ. *Direction increases corporate efficiency in two distinct ways.* The prayer of the parish—which is the local manifestation of the complete Body—is obviously enhanced by the progress of its individual members, but apart from this, direction discovers and develops dormant gifts which can be directly used for the good of all. It may well be, for example, that a particular soul has just that gift for intercessory prayer which the Vicar can use in his ministry to the whole parish. But only personal direction is likely to make it effective; first by awakening the latent gift and then, if the director concerned is not the parish priest himself, by effecting the necessary introduction and knowledge to that parish priest. One does not normally approach the Vicar with "Do you realize what a remarkably gifted person I am, Father?" Whatever our gifts or aspirations we usually leave our coach, guide, or mentor to boast about them. But nor must we sink to mock-modesty (which is quite the reverse of humility) by the stubborn insistence that we have no gifts at all. Proficiency implies that most of us try to serve the Church worthily in a quiet and humble way, but the fact remains that God is much more lavish with his gifts than many people suppose. To deny that is neither humble nor reverent.

Many a parish priest is like a cricketer who is asked to captain "Somebody's XI" made up of players from all over the country, all unknown to him and to one another. He probably has a pretty good team but no one knows who are the batsmen and who are the bowlers, and having led the side to an ignoble defeat, he discovers that the quiet little man who has been doing nothing on the boundary all day is Jones of Warwickshire who would almost certainly have broken the big stand earlier on. If only he had known, if only he had been told: how much practical, usable spiritual power lies latent in our parishes because the Vicar does not know? because of the lack of direction?

(2) I am trying, however unsuccessfully, to abide by my principle that theology should be applied, not merely taught; and that there is no point in bothering busy people with more doctrine than is strictly necessary. That is why I dislike the term "instructed Christians"—it implies people who absorb knowledge without using it. But of course this is not *my* principle but the general tenet of the Church: *that holiness and sanctity, not to mention simple proficiency, do not depend on intellect.* But this involves direction, because if doctrine is to be applied to the needs of unique souls someone must apply it, and only a personal director can do that.

The very practical outcome is that direction saves you the trouble of struggling with a lot of theology; it *can* save you from bothering with it at all. I think the modern tendency, and it is a very healthy one, is to ask for reasons instead of, or at least as well as, authority. I assume that the majority of people aiming at proficiency desire some understanding of what the Faith really is and what membership of the Body of Christ means; that is the assumption behind this book. But there is still a minority who by temperament, lack of intellect, or possession of a different sort of intellect, simply cannot be bothered with doctrine; perhaps some have floundered through Chapter 2 without much satisfaction, in which case I hope they have ploughed on as far as this. Because to them I would say: "It does not matter a scrap—*so long as you seek direction.* Find a capable priest, explain the position, put yourself under his care, and do as you are told!" That is *not* autocracy, priestcraft, or any such thing, but a common-sense arrangement for a particular type of soul, who does not want to be cluttered up with theology. It is a free choice of alternatives: if you are so inclined, learn, discuss, argue, demand all the reasons why—that is very healthy; but if you are not so inclined, then seek direction and get on with it.

But we must bear in mind St Bernard's blunt statement at the head of this chapter. All the theology there is would be insufficient to direct ourselves, for the very commonplace reason that we cannot see ourselves. The golfer, "plus-man" or "rabbit" it makes no difference, can spend fruitless hours alone trying to cure a fault in his play. If he is wise he goes to the club professional and says, "*Watch* me play this stroke and *tell me where I go wrong.*" And that is direction.

(3) *Direction frees us from the tyranny of feeling.* Emotion plays a good, rightful, and important part in religious life, private prayer without any feeling at all would be unbearable for most of us, but emotion and feeling must be disciplined and understood. That is why all the great classics of the spiritual life contain large sections on "the discernment of spirits", to use the technical term. And in unique souls, each with his own characteristics and traits, feeling is the most capricious element of all. It would take volumes even to attempt a classification, but luckily we do not need volumes; we are served well enough for practical purposes by direction itself. The one vital point for us is simply this: it cannot be said too often that the only certain guide to spiritual progress is moral theology—we are making progress in prayer when we commit fewer sins. Nevertheless, God in his goodness and wisdom sends us consolations and spiritual experiences which we find joyful and exciting. It would be shocking to deny or discount them. The trouble is that we can misuse, or become greedy for, these things as we can any other of God's good gifts. Food, drink, pleasure, sex, games, and spiritual emotion, are all good things; gluttony, for *any* of them, remains one of the capital sins. All of which gives the devil and ourselves every chance to go astray, and to become incapable of prayer without feeling is as bad as being incapable of life without beer. It can be a terrible addiction.

In this context, and with an almost absurd simplicity, it must suffice to mention four main types of feeling that the ordinary Christian will most likely encounter. First, there are bad feelings, the literal and direct work of the devil; feelings in prayer which positively mislead us and suggest methods or aspects of prayer that would be really harmful. Secondly, there are feelings which are good and pleasant; which spur us on to greater effort, and encourage us to joyful thanksgiving. But of course there is danger here, we can be greedy and demand more than God's wisdom chooses to give, and we can put too much reliance on them and be tempted to test our progress by them: a completely false criterion. Thirdly, there are feelings which are good and unpleasant; these can be most creative if used and interpreted rightly, yet they can do us harm if we allow them to worry us too much. Fourth, are what we might call "prophetic" feelings, when we think God is giving us some definite instruction—when we feel "led by the Spirit". Sometimes he is, sometimes he is not; sometimes we are, sometimes we are not. If we are *sure* that God has spoken to us then we must obey, but how often are we *sure* all by ourselves? Do not forget that reason and "conscience", in a vacuum, are no more reliable than feeling itself. Any parish priest will tell of a quite remarkable number of instances where the "Holy Spirit" has given explicit orders contrary to Our Lord's ordinances and to the doctrine of his Church!

Prayer is an adventure, there is a sense in which we must take risks, but there is no virtue in being foolhardy. So share these experiences with a competent director, or at least share them with some reasonably experienced Christian, here if anywhere two heads are better than one.

(4) Anglican direction is always inclined to be "empirical" rather than "dogmatic"; it includes guidance, experiment, argument, and free discussion, it is a mutual working out of ways and means for personal development. Anglican priests are not despotic—and if you find one who is, you can always seek another and I would strongly advise you to do so—they guide, they do not command. But there is still the good, strong traditional virtue of *Holy obedience*, which in no way contravenes Anglican liberties. The operative word is "Holy";

obedience is strictly amoral which can be good, bad, or indifferent according to what is obeyed and why. *Holy* obedience is the expression of that humility which convinces us that we might be wrong; that our thoughts, conscience, and especially feelings, might lead us astray. It is the principle behind my "lowest efficient method of going to Church" described in Chapter 3. If despite distraction, boredom, inattention, and sluggishness, we go to Mass, we are adding something to the action of the Church simply by "being there". And we are adding something, however little, to our personal progress; given a modicum of good-will, what we lose in devotion we make up by obedience. We have shown that the life of the Christian is both corporate and personal, and both aspects are very closely related. The dictates of the Church, like being at Mass on certain days, are clear enough, there can be no doubt about our duty; but the personal decisions of everyday life can be much more complicated. Are we really doing enough by way of prayer? Is our Rule, or our penance, or our almsgiving, sufficient? We feel tired and listless and dull; shall we struggle on in prayer or have a little rest? Many moral decisions of life seem to consist of straight alternatives; which ought we to choose? And most difficult of all: was that experience in prayer true or false, does it mean this or that, am I being "led by the Spirit" or by something very very different indeed?

Now what applies to the soul incorporated into Christ's Body applies also to the priesthood; the priest is the representative of the corporate Church, as at the Eucharist, but he can also be its personal representative to individual souls. A great many of the queries in the last paragraph tend to solve themselves in direction and I think that should be the normal way, but as a last resort the onus of decision can be put on to the director. Obviously this can be overdone but, *as a last resort*, Christians need not suffer those agonies of indecision so common in modern life. After a mutual struggle with a problem they can say to their director: "Look here, I am sorry but I simply cannot make up my mind about this thing, will you please tell me what to do?" The priest is as weak, sinful, worried, and incompetent as anyone else; he might ask permission to consult another—three heads are better than two—and, after all this, it might look as if he had decided wrongly. The vital thing is that the problem has been lifted out of the rut of expediency on to the heights of Holy obedience: action following such a decision may not work out as we had hoped but it cannot be "wrong", it cannot be sinful. Rather than oppressive tyranny, direction can give a most glorious freedom.

(5) In some ways most important of all, though more subtle and difficult to explain, is the fact that *the actual relation in direction*, the relation of spiritual Father to spiritual son or daughter, *is itself creative.*[1] It is subtle because it is unique and no single analogy is adequate to explain it. The traditional idea of a priest as physician of the soul teaches a great deal but it fails at one crucial point; doctors cure disease, they are only consulted in case of sickness, hence direction takes on a negative, over moral, aspect. It is true that direction and sacramental confession often go together, but they need not and they are certainly not the same thing; that would be making the greater equal to the less. In this context—I will deal with it more generally in Chapter 9—Confession is a useful, normal but comparatively small part of the whole process of direction.

(And here might I make a rather impertinent plea to both parties, that despite the connection, confession and direction be properly distinguished in practice? Confessional counsel should surely be most strictly confined to the content of the actual confession; to particular sins which cannot be mentioned elsewhere. And the penitent, in turn, should not "confess" normal general tendencies like distraction and aridity which are not sins, but the matter of direction. The confessional is not the place for a general debate, nor for dealing with things that could be discussed more easily and more comfortably in an arm-chair by the fire.)

The "ascetic" analogy, of coach or trainer of the spiritual athlete, supplies the necessary positive aspect. It suggests no

[1] As Guibert says (*The Theology of the Spiritual Life*, p. 171): "God showers many graces on souls who seek direction, even though the director may tell them nothing that they did not already know."

mere restoring to health but the purposeful turning of strength into skill. A combination of these ideas takes us a little further, but they both fail at another crucial point: direction is a *mutual* thing, a two-way relation. It is true that a doctor gains something in experience with each case, and the coach develops his special art with practice; but the spiritual director gains immeasurably more than that. Here are two souls joined in mutual support, in a mutual quest, to the greater glory of God, and the redemption of the world. They are bound together in the intimacy of the sacred humanity of Christ, and they support one another continually by a type of intercession which does not depend on any particular "prayers". This is, in the best possible sense, a *personal relation*, involving joy, suffering, and sacrifice. The bond involved is the bond of Love, and no other word is adequate to describe it. Perhaps after all the best analogy of this relation is that between Father and son or daughter—it is the most obvious illustration of all, but let us try to improve on it by putting them all together in the family business.

II

It is not surprising that so subtle a relation involves certain pitfalls and demands certain precautions; nor indeed that it is so frequently misunderstood. So at the risk of some deviation I feel that a little straight thinking on the whole subject might be wise. The fact of the matter is that the serious, sincere, and creative guidance of one Christian soul by another often gives rise to emotional aspects which are by no means unnatural or unhealthy. In fact some sense of trust, respect, and even affection, may add much to the strength and progress of both parties. On the other hand, here as in any other human relation, things occasionally go wrong and scandal arises; which, needless to say, is both exaggerated and misinterpreted by the less reputable sections of the press. The idea of Christian efficiency itself demands that the question be squarely faced.

In the first place, I do not think the Church is very well served by a small group of priests and writers who insist that this relation is "impersonal"; it is untrue, it denies a great deal of tradition, and logically, of course, an impersonal relation between persons is a contradiction in terms. What is really meant by this evasion is that it is a special kind of relation; which is perfectly true if equally ambiguous.

A little progress is made by those who are bold enough to bring in the word Love, but, abused as this glorious word is, it still seems curious that the very first-fruits of the Christian religion should need so much apology. Christian love we are reminded is firstly the love of Christ for men, thence secondly, the love of men and women for one another in Christ; and it is something that demands will before emotion and service before feeling. That again is quite true, but it is more true than the evasive school cares to admit for this familiar Christian teaching is concerned with priorities not alternatives; emotion, feeling, trust, and attraction are of minor importance, but they cannot be left out altogether. The crux of the matter seems to be that Christianity also teaches the solidarity of human personality wherein *all* experience contains elements of *all* our characteristics: mind, body, spirit, senses, emotion, feeling, will, and, of course, sex. The question is of such importance that I think it really demands a study in itself, by one far more competent to make it than myself. Here it must suffice to look very briefly at four aspects of this relationship; the ascetical tradition of the Church, psychology, theology, and lastly and meditatively at Our Lord himself. It can certainly do not harm to air a problem so frequently evaded.

The consensus of opinion of the Saints provide two facts and one ambiguity. First, as is not the case with parish priests or diocesan bishops, spiritual directors are freely chosen by the individuals concerned. In its most rigorous moods and ages, the Church has always allowed, and even encouraged, this freedom of choice; and it is impossible to grant personal choice and deny a personal relation. Secondly, in contrast to our own broad-minded anaemia, the Saints have a most refreshing habit of calling a spade a spade; they are not frightened of words like love, affection, and friendship. St Teresa is the last woman in the world to be led into a false emotionalism, yet she can write:

"I intend treating of two kinds of love: one which is entirely spiritual, free from any sort of affection or natural tenderness which could tarnish its purity, and another which is spiritual but mingled with the frailty and weakness of human nature. The latter is good and seems lawful, being such as is felt between relatives and friends, and is that which I have mentioned before. The first of these two ways of loving, and the one that I will discuss, is unmixed with any kind of passion that would disturb its harmony. This love, exercised with moderation and discretion, is profitable in every way, particularly when borne towards holy people and confessors, for that which seems only natural is then changed into virtue. At times, however, these two kinds of love seem so combined that it is difficult to distinguish them from one another, especially as regards a confessor. When persons who practise prayer discover that their confessor is a holy man who understands their spiritual state, they feel a strong affection for him; the devil then opens a perfect battery of scruples on the soul, which, as he intends, greatly disturb it, especially if the priest is leading his penitent to higher perfection. Then the evil one torments his victim to such a pitch that she leaves her director, so that the temptation gives her no peace either in one way or the other.

"In such a case it is best not to think about whether you like your confessor or not, or whether you wish to like him. If we feel friendship for those who benefit our bodies, why should we not feel as great a friendship for those who strive and labour to benefit our souls? On the contrary, I think a liking for my confessor is a great help to my progress if he is holy and spiritual, and I see that he endeavours to profit my soul. Human nature is so weak that this feeling is often a help to our undertaking great things in God's service."

St Teresa, in her wisdom and common sense, has here unearthed the real danger. Our pastoral relations go wrong because we do not try to understand and face up to them. The evil is not that a close pastoral relation of love is wrong, but that the scruples of the devil (and the newspapers) make us think that it might be. We become inhibited through ignorance and frustrated by un-Christian convention. St Teresa continues: "If, however, the confessor[1] be a man of

[1] Note that St Teresa uses *Confessor* and *Director* interchangeably.

indifferent character, we must not let him know of our liking for him." Even in such unsatisfactory circumstances, calling for wise precaution, there is still nothing wrong with the love itself!

We now come to the ambiguity, which seems to bother St Teresa as much as it bothers me. What does she really mean by "spiritual love"? It is a common enough expression in medieval ascetic—from which it is obviously borrowed in the passage above—and I would guess that St Teresa's rather clumsy attempt to combine her two kinds of love is no more than an admission of her dissatisfaction with the original term. Can any human relation be completely free from "the frailty and weakness of human nature"? I think it must be admitted that medieval psychology, though nearer the truth than some modern schools of thought suppose, was in error at some points. Integrated personality was at least *explained* in terms of disparate "faculties"; Manichaeism—the heresy that matter is intrinsically evil—had frequently to be repulsed from ascetical thought.

But the medieval mind was not, in the strict sense, Puritan; it was sacramental. It would be much more at home with the idea of the "spiritual body" than with the Puritan "spirit" without any body. And of course "spiritual" could mean "religious" or "holy". I suggest that "spiritual love" is either a Puritan impossibility—like an impersonal personal relation—or it means "religious love", or "holy love" or even simply "good love". What it cannot possibly mean is "ordinary" love minus all semblance of feeling, emotion, and excitement. It cannot mean "Platonic" love, which in popular use really means a particular kind of ordinary love and in classical use means something rather unhealthy.

More up-to-date psychology helps considerably for it springs from the firm dogma of integrated personality (which is only Biblical psychology more adequately expressed). Here all human experience concerns the whole human person; experiences can only be classified as mental, physical, religious, or emotional in so far as all the things in our complex make-up vary in proportion, but they are all included in every experience.

This is the crux of the matter. When it is recognized that the mind plays its part in eating and drinking and that the human "spirit" has something to do with recovery from a broken leg, then nothing human can be omitted from prayer, direction, and the relations involved. No one will quibble if I say that all pastoral relations are qualified by a "love of souls" but a "soul" is an embodied person not a disembodied "spirit" and the dangers of this common misinterpretation are two-fold. First, an exaggerated fear of "attachment"—which St Teresa bluntly calls scrupulous—gives rise to that unattractive clerical crust which laymen not unreasonably find hard to penetrate. Secondly, if some sort of relation is achieved it invaribly hardens into a pompous authoritarianism wholly opposed to the warm domestic tone inherent in the English pastoral tradition. "By this shall all men know that ye are my disciples, if you have love one to another" suggests a perfectly obvious manifestation of love rather than a cold impersonal secret. Now we are incorporated into the glorified humanity of Christ by Baptism; we are made members of him and of one another. His humanity is full, perfect, and complete; all the relations and inter-relations are of love. Creation and redemption are both acts of the love of God freely flowing to the whole world and to all persons. That is the universal aspect, but what of the personal and pastoral? What example does Christ give to us? If we face the implications of meditative prayer enlightened by Christology, we reach conclusions that some will find shocking: but I cannot help that. Jesus Christ is perfect Man, *a* perfect Man, "like unto us in all things, sin except". What then were his feelings, emotions, and reactions, when the beloved disciple rested his head on his breast at supper? and when Magdalene wept over his feet and caressed them with her hair? when he shed tears for Lazarus and embraced children? To call this "impersonal" is not only Puritan, not only Apollinarian, but blasphemous.

All I wish to say, and I apologize for taking so long to say it, is that as some are so scared of alcohol that they form total abstinence societies, so some ascetical writers are so scared of "attachment" that they eradicate love, warmth, and friendship. A priest should have more and not less concern, care, and love for his family in God than has a doctor for his patients or a lawyer for his clients; in fact it consists of brothers and sisters in Christ and not "cases". Moreover the "family" aspect, the work, honour, and proficiency of the local Body, should be a safeguard rather than a danger.

III

Let us now suppose that the ordinary Christian, seeking proficiency, has decided that spiritual direction is a normal and necessary thing, and that he has made up his mind to try the experiment. What exactly does he do? I think it would be simplest if I were allowed to address some straightforward advice directly to such a person.

(1) The Church gives you absolute freedom of choice as to who your director shall be. Your parish priest may well be the right person and this arrangement has added advantages, but there is no question of obligation, and should you go elsewhere it involves no disloyalty or insult. The priesthood rightly contains great variety; some of us can do one job and others have different gifts. Your parish priest may be a great Old Testament scholar, a good administrator, and a fine preacher, but he may be—despite deep personal devotion—bored to tears with the technology of prayer. And this *is* a personal relation where trust and temperament have rightful places. Some people are happier with a close social relation in direction—inevitable with your own incumbent—and some prefer their director to be rather outside normal life—a more plainly professional relation. You have free choice.

(2) But use your free choice rightly: and you will not go very far wrong if you follow St Teresa. Give absolute priority to *competence*, which means a working knowledge of ascetical and moral theology supported by a regular life of prayer. As in all things a small minority have a special gift for the direction of souls, if you are lucky enough to find such a specialist there is no more to be said, but plain competence is the only essential. Do not seek the ideal, do not be too fussy. Secondly, and still in accord with St Teresa, do not *fear* "attractiveness" implying someone whose judgement you think you can trust, someone you find approachable and easy to talk to. Here

we can apply the medical analogy exactly; your doctor must be qualified and competent, if he is also a respected friend so much the better. You do not choose him because you like the colour of his eyes yet there is no virtue in having a doctor or priest just because you hate the sight of him.

Never forget the primary purpose of the whole thing: a partnership to the glory of God and the more efficient furtherance of his work by personal progress. A partnership truly "in Christ" is rather obviously going to create love between the partners. That is not "wrong" but the essential fruit of the Christian Faith. Follow St Teresa and stop worrying about the scruples of the devil.

We must nevertheless accept rather than evade "the frailty and weakness of human nature". Of course we must fight and guard against sin in *every* occasion and relation of daily life. But we must also guard against inefficiency, particularly in this present context; and this flows not from love, respect, and affection, but from what the text-books call "attachment". St Ignatius teaches that man is "to make use of creatures (which of course includes directors of souls) just so far as they help him to attain his end (to praise, reverence, and serve God our Lord) and to withdraw himself from them just so far as they hinder him". Quite simply our general love and benevolence towards the creation, and our more particular love for our fellow Christians and those close to us; all flow from our love for God in Christ. So however healthy the bond of love in direction, it must ever be strictly subservient to the increase of our love for Christ. If, however unwittingly, a director "replaces" or "gets in the way of" the soul's intercourse with God, then something has gone wrong; not because the relation is intrinsically evil or scandalous but because it is inefficient. And there is a perfectly simple test: as direction itself is the efficient technique of prayer, so its bond of love can be a spur to our effort; it can almost be described as a sacramental thing—it has its own material and spiritual aspects. So if difficulty, sloth, failing, or sin, cause any *particular* reticence or embarrassment in our approach to a *particular* priest then something is wrong. If we feel we are failing *him* and not God, if our weaknesses and frailty seem worse in the eyes of one priest above others, then inefficiency creeps in. Conversely, if a Director becomes more worried over the sins and faults of one spiritual child than he is over the *same* sins and faults in another; then things are not as they should be. If that is a pronounced initial feeling on either side, it will not be a satisfactory partnership, and if it becomes pronounced during such a relationship, then it may be wise to break it. Again not so much because of evil but because of inefficiency; not because there is too much love but because there is not enough. Your director is always and wholly, come what may, "on your side"—if that is not apparent, something is wrong. Real love for a father means complete openness in all circumstances, as soon as we wish to hide things from him, for whatever motive, there is not enough love of the right sort.

Although this is an obvious safeguard, it is as well to dispose of the incredible amount of nonsense we hear about priesthood, direction, and sacraments, "hindering" or "coming between" the "direct approach of the soul to God". In face of the Incarnation, the sacraments, the Church, our own sin and the ineffable glory of God; it is quite unbelievable that any sane man really thinks that he can simply kneel down on the back lawn and achieve perfect union with God. It is the most arrogant nonsense imaginable, and I do not know how many heresies besides. "Mediation" is fundamental to the Christmas story and all that flows from it, and a mediator (the very core of priesthood) is surely someone who brings things together rather than separates them? If Brown introduces Jones to Smith I fail to see how he can be keeping them apart; a letter certainly "comes between" two correspondents, but as a link not a barrier.

Now my own experience, for what it is worth, is that God not infrequently forges this relation himself. It simply happens that in ordinary parochial life, or by addresses, or in retreat; we begin to realize that a certain priest is the right person to help us. And conversely: I think most spiritual directors, in normal parish life, get a pretty good idea as to whom they might be of service long before any such relation is established. God draws them together as he did St Paul and Timothy or St François de Sales and Madame de Chantal; St Paul talks of his own spiritual children (in terms of endearment the English parish would find quite shocking) as "begotten in the Lord" meaning obviously "re-born by Baptism" but also I think "nurtured and brought up in Christ". In fact the term "Father" is rather more than a High Church affectation!

All this leads up to a vital practical point: however you choose, or whoever you choose, as your director, *you must make the first move*, and in direction, whenever you want particular help *you must ask for it.* Whatever priests may do in the name of evangelism, it would be arrogant and quite intolerable for them to say to anyone, "I think *I* ought to be your spiritual director!" Priests must be, in practice, self-effacing and reticent. It would be impossible and against all etiquette for a doctor to stop you in the street with "My word you look ill, you had better come to my surgery". It would be as bad for the family doctor, however much of a friend, to call occasionally just to be sure you were quite well. And there is nothing worse than the sort of priestly possessiveness that is for ever popping in to see if "everything is going all right"! That attitude only shows up lack of trust, lack of manners, over-anxiety, and lack of love. *Therefore you must make the first move—always.*

(3) But do not be too fussy. Competence is the only essential. So if the associations of ordinary life fail, consult your Christian friends or clergy in exactly the same way as you seek a dentist when you are in a strange district. If that fails write to anyone you like who is in a position to advise, if need be to the Bishop; you can be assured that you are not "troubling" anyone with something trivial. I have no direct experience of episcopal emotions, but I venture an inspired guess that a letter seeking a spiritual guide, amongst all the finances, speeches, committees, awkward churchwardens, and more awkward clergymen, would at least be a refreshing change.

Having found an adequate guide somehow:

(4) *Use him.* Remember it is a two-way relation, do not be apologetic, you cannot be a "nuisance"—unless you are downright foolish. It is sometimes just a little difficult to decide precisely when, and when not, to consult a director.

The medical analogy helps here too; you do not rush off to the doctor with every slight cold or headache—direction is not "submissive" and you must stand before God on your own two feet—but do not wait until pneumonia is firmly set in. If we bring in the dentist, we have the idea of the regular periodic examination, which is a normal practice in direction and a very sensible one. But do not feel tied to such an arrangement, and *you* must still make the request—every time.

(5) Do not fear if you find it difficult to talk about spiritual things; either because of reticence—prayer is a "normal" thing, much more so than having chunks of tooth bored out—or because you find spiritual experience hard to express in words. You are not expected to be an expert in ascetical theology, which is the whole point of consulting someone who is; a big part of the job is helping people who "don't quite know how to put it, Father". After all, "I have a pain—here" is a fairly adequate statement to the doctor; after that it is his business to diagnose and prescribe.

(6) Direction entails "no obligation" either to follow the priest's counsel or to continue with the relation. The doctor helps again; there is no point in consulting anyone you do not trust and whose advice you do not intend to follow, but do not worry if you forget something and do not be afraid to argue: this is an empirical relation of love in Christ, not an interview with the headmaster. Do not change priests too often, do not flit from one to another—that implies a sort of spiritual hypochondria—but, worse still, never reach the stage when you feel that nobody else will do, that is "attachment". Sometime someone else will have to do.

(7) Direction frequently includes confession, but it need not. In any case direction can be carried out efficiently (sometimes more efficiently) by letter. Confession can not! Therefore your director and confessor can be two different priests, and your parish priest can be a third. Here all the relations can become a bit complicated, but not so badly as it sounds. In any case if your director and, or, confessor is not your parish priest, the latter should be told of the relation. Parochial efficiency demands that the parish priest should know what is going on (see pp. 26–7 *supra*). The matter of direction is not

strictly "under the seal" but it entails ordinary professional confidence. The parish priest should not want to know any details, but it will help him to know that you are a Proficient or "Regular" under direction, and not just "rather a keen churchman". In the event of conflict, the needs of the parish come before the needs of the individual; the efficient working of the local Body takes precedence over the details of a personal Rule.

(8) Last but by no means least, seek direction in prayer when things are going well; when you are cool, calm, and collected—or rather recollected. Prayer is a positive adventure not a negative duty. Human nature, and the unfortunate "medieval-medical" equating of direction with confession; all lead to the idea that you put off consulting a priest until you are in the throes of serious aridity, trouble, or sin. It is much easier for a priest to help you when all is well, and such guidance lived out in prayer will hold you in good stead when difficulty or trouble arise. All parish priests have seen the frustration and fear in those who suddenly seek consolation from prayer and religion in bereavement; the callous but true answer is that they should have got down to the matter twelve months earlier. If you are on a sinking ship in the middle of the ocean, it is a bit late to learn to swim. Look on prayer in terms of adventure and proficiency at least as well as devotion. Do not wait for disaster.

IV

Two small but important points remain. In certain parochial centres, and in books, especially American, there has recently arisen an activity known as "counselling" or "pastoral counselling", or even "extra-confessional counselling". This *could* mean direction (in which case why not say so?), but it is usually something very different. It seems mainly to be concerned with the immediate problems of practical life with an emphasis on those in trouble: broken marriages, crime, immorality (I use the word widely and correctly not in the ludicrously genteel sense), destitution, mental disturbance, and so on. It bases its advice on Christian teaching of a somewhat liberal kind, and makes much use of psychology and psychiatry. Its "counsellors" include priests, doctors, and welfare workers, and I think it deals mainly with isolated cases of distress, therefore its relationships are normally short-lived; when the problem is solved the job is done, though there may be a strong evangelistic aspect. Now this kind of help may fulfil an important social need, it is charity in the real sense, and a good work for Christians to undertake. But it is plainly nothing whatever to do with the direction of souls, and my only quarrel with it is in its flagrant, and possibly very dangerous, misuse of terms. The word "counsel" is deep-rooted in orthodox tradition; we speak of the "evangelical counsels" and ask our confessor for "penance, counsel, and absolution". I take this to imply a semi-technical term meaning particular direction based on some definite body of knowledge, it is not just general advice. In legal terms "counsel" is a trained lawyer who interprets law, not a friend who gives his own opinion. So in confession we ask the priest to interpret our sin and give counsel based on moral theology, not on his private view of the matter. (I maintain that "advice" here is quite the wrong word.) Now I do not wish to attack brothers in Christ who are doing charitable work, nor to enter into a pedantic quibble over words. The fact remains that, to the uninitiated, "pastoral counselling" sounds very much as if it ought to be spiritual direction; guidance in prayer, over a long period, positive, and based entirely on ascetical and moral theology: which is exactly what it is not. It would be quite dreadful if a Christian who really wanted direction presented himself for "counselling".

The second point is that sermons, schools of prayer, retreat addresses, and so on, play their time-honoured part in the integrated Christian life, but these too have little to do with direction; they are certainly no substitute for it. If you want to know how to prune pear trees, you do not rush round to a public lecture on fruit-growing in the vague hope that the subject will crop up and be "helpful". You go and ask someone. Yet a good many do tend to use sermons in that way—and criticize the preacher.

In the event of conflict between, say, retreat addresses, and direction, give precedence to the latter, or at least work the thing out with your director. This does not mean that either of them is "wrong". It is good and right that the Church should embrace such rich diversity of prayer; of schools, methods, and modes. It would be pretty dull if all retreats were strictly Ignatian or strictly Franciscan, or strictly anything else. But one soul's prayer must be a consistent whole; a "rule" of prayer consisting of various little hints and tenets, picked up at random from here and there, would be too dreadful for words. Given a firm basis, the little hints can be fitted in and used creatively; which is another good reason in favour of direction itself.[1]

[1] See further on this important subject: Guibert, *The Theology of the Spiritual Life*, pp. 155–86.

5

RULE

Multiplication is vexation,
Division is as bad,
The Rule of Three doth puzzle me
And Practice drives me mad.

Trad. nursery rhyme

I

"RULE" IS the literal translation of the Latin word *regula*—rule, pattern, model, example—from which we derive "Regular" as both noun and adjective. Both words are technical terms of ascetical theology associated with, but by no means exclusive to, St Benedict, and they present the same little problem as we found with "direction"; their meaning is not quite the same as that of common use. Rule, like pattern, model, or system, is an essentially *singular* word, in some ways directly opposite to a list of "rules", and a "Regular" Christian is one who "lives to Rule". We find this term in the "Regular clergy" or "Canons Regular" and it implies much the same as when we speak of a Regular soldier in the Regular army; not so much one who keeps a lot of rules or who is strictly disciplined but an efficient full-time professional. If we may stretch the analogy a little a Regular layman is one who embraces the Christian life as opposed to the keen "territorial" who goes to church fairly often and tries to say his prayers now and again. It implies status more than quality, efficiency more than keenness or brilliance; volunteers and conscripts *might* prove to be braver and more zealous than regular soldiers but they are unlikely to be more generally proficient. So it must be admitted that Rule is not absolutely essential to creative and progressive Christian life —there is a minority, I think a very small one, of those temperamentally unsuited to embrace Rule—but in general to be a Regular and to be a Proficient comes to much the same thing.

Because this principle is so widely misunderstood, we must try to clear up some of the common errors before we get down to the practical matter of constructing and using Rule. But let it be said at once that Rule is a help and not a hindrance, something liberating not restrictive, expansive not burdensome, in accord with the freedom of the Christian spirit and absolutely opposed to "legalism". It is *always* the means to an end and *never* an end in itself, and its content is *only* ascetical theology. In civilized life we make much use—more than is generally recognized—of all sorts of little disciplines, habits and rules; we might get up at a certain hour, always shave before breakfast, never be seen out with dirty shoes, and take a drink only at weekends, and I believe the Boy Scouts try to perform one good deed a day. All that is wise and good but we must be quite clear that it has nothing whatever to do with Rule in its proper sense. (Personally, although this is debatable, I would go so far as to say that almsgiving and fasting are not strictly matters of Rule[1]; the former is subsidiary to thanksgiving and the latter is inextricably bound up with Recollection—this does not of course mean that these laudable customs should not be subject to "rules". Again as mere opinion, I think we should avoid the ambiguous term "Rule of *Life*" for "Rule of *Prayer*" or better still just Rule. Either these are synonyms or the former involves a quite different non-ascetical principle. But that is rather a quibble.) The starting point is that Rule implies order, and if "Order is Heav'n's first law" its opposite is not liberty but chaos. Lack of Rule means not freedom of spirit but confusion. Let us then examine five very common misconceptions.

(1) *Rule is "embraced" not "promised".* It would be Pharisaical, legalistic and quite unchristian solemnly to promise to "keep" a Rule; and it would involve the sin of pride and the heresy of Pelagianism at least. In any case you can only "keep" a lot of little rules. A Christian Regular is one who

[1] See pages 21, 54.

chooses to undertake his common obligations and duties, and to develop his personal spirituality, by acknowledging, accepting or "embracing" some total scheme, system, pattern or "Rule" of prayer. Setting aside all the subtleties and technical ramifications of the Religious life, strictly so called, I think it can be said that in general, the novice "takes his vows" only with regard to the evangelical counsels, which, together with the Rule of his community, he "embraces" as the foundation of a particular type of life. He has then made a decision not to marry, own property, or defy the general authority of his Order, but however unchaste he is, however covetous—even to the extent of robbery—and however disobedient; he can only literally "break his vow" by returning to the world. Nor does he solemnly promise to keep his Rule and never break it; again he can only "break" it by returning to the world. However bad a monk may be, so long as he remains in his community he is still a monk. (It is chastening to realize here, that because there is no specific sacramental act involved, a Religious may be dispensed from his vow, and this is nothing like so impossible or scandalous as what we call "divorce" or what is implied by a "lapsed communicant".)

So a Christian lay-Regular is one who intends, and attempts, to order his life of prayer in a particular way, according to some clear-cut model. He may do it well or badly, he may fail seldom or often (and as we shall see, there is little direct connection between "well" and "seldom", "badly" and "often") but he can only "break" his Rule, or cease to be a Regular, by giving up the whole principle of the thing.

(2) *Rule is wholly opposed to legalism.* Let us look at one or two concrete examples. A man embraces a particular Rule in Lent which, in this special case, includes a complete fast from tobacco. His motive, the end for which Rule is the means, is to deepen his spiritual life, to grow somewhat in the Love of God, decrease his sins, make a definite renunciation of the pleasure of tobacco and offer it to God, and give its value to a missionary society. On Ash-Wednesday night he smokes a cigarette: what does this mean? The Pharisee would say that he had "broken" his Rule and that was that—very shocking

—but having "failed" he might as well give the whole thing up, let his prayer slip back to normal and smoke whenever he wishes. By the principle of Rule, on the other hand, this man is just as much of a true Regular after his smoke as he was before, all that has happened is that he has made a minor "fault". He would simply carry on with his Rule; it would be quite wrong to speak of his "starting again" for that would imply that something had been irrevocably "lost". And on Holy Saturday he would look back, calmly, casually and with not so very much interest, to recognize that he has to admit to twenty or thirty "faults" including eight cigarettes. He may find that his besetting sin is curiously under control, his others are reduced, and that the fruits of two or three particularly inspiring meditations are still much in his life; he will make his Easter communion with great joy and give the missionary society one and sixpence less than it might have had. Now only the very silliest sort of legalist would say that this man had not "kept Lent", only the most bigoted could say that Rule had nothing to do with his progress, or that he could have achieved the same without it. And only the blindest of Pharisees could ask, "What is the point of a Rule if you break it?" And the last to criticize would be the missionary society.

Now let us suppose that this man has managed without any faults at all. First, how pleased the Pharisee will be! how enthusiastic in his congratulation and how pleased with such "success". But the man most concerned, if he is the Christian Regular I take him to be, will quietly ask himself precisely the same fundamental questions; "has my prayer really deepened and expanded? have my sins diminished? have I grown in the Love of God and expressed it in my life? He will most likely realize that his Rule is largely responsible for the affirmative answers; apart from that his keeping of Rule without fault is of no importance whatsoever: it is merely the means to an end.

Or suppose that there are so many faults that he can barely be said to have kept the Rule at all? Again the basic questions of moral and ascetical theology are the only ones that matter; and, although experience suggests that in this case the answers are probably, though not certainly, negative, the man is still a Regular just as much as in the preceding example. He is still "embracing Rule" unless or until he firmly and decisively rejects the whole principle of Rule itself. In fact, the keeping of Rule so badly may well pin-point some unrecognized weakness or difficulty, so that it may be set right and he is spurred on to further effort.

If the Pharisee persists with his parrot-cry: "What is the good of Rule if you keep on breaking it?" or more subtly, "If it does not matter if you break Rule what is the point of having it?", then the final answer is that contained in the heading of this sub-section. Rule is just not intended for legalists, it is completely incompatible with that type of outlook: it presupposes a soul enlightened by the living Spirit of Christ, it has no use at all for the dead letter of the law.

It may still be argued that it might be simpler, just to try to do one's best without Rule at all. In that case—apart from the fact that I do not quite know how one "does one's best" without something just a little more definite—one of two things is bound to happen. The scrupulous or even conscientious person will tend to discount his own weakness (which is pride) and take on far too much. He will never satisfy his own conscience, pray himself to a standstill, or into chronic aridity, and confront Holy Saturday with nothing more creative than a nervous breakdown (which will doubtless be called religious mania). The lax person, and I fear this is the more likely alternative, will simply slip back into a dull and dormant mediocrity.

(3) *Rule is neither artificial nor a burden, but the principle of civilized life.* It is not unreasonable to be a little irked by the daily rush to catch the 8.15 to work and the 5.45 home, to clock in at 7 prompt, and to swallow a well-earned pint because it is nearly closing time. It is not unreasonable because most of these daily nuisances are rather tedious little rules. Nevertheless, those tied by such restrictions have sometimes made the holiday experiment known as "getting away from it all". They decide, amongst other things, to eat when they happen to feel like it, what they happen to fancy at the time—and away with the conventions. In practice, the

burden of deciding if you really want steak and kidney pie for breakfast, or whether you are quite hungry enough ta bother to cook, or whether dinner at midnight is really quite such fun; becomes so intolerable that after about three days everything is back to normal. Rule is seen to have so many advantages over "freedom". We are back with the old enemy, *feeling*. What is so exacting is not the facing of responsible decisions but being cluttered up with a host of petty and unnecessary ones. Breakfast, lunch and dinner, at 8, 1, and 7, with occasional variations, is so much the easier and better way. Rule that stipulates Mass on, say, Sundays, Wednesdays and Saints' days, is so much easier than the irksome, perennial "Is it not about time I made my communion? or perhaps next Friday will do?"

(4) *Breach of Rule is not sin.* This is plain from the foregoing, but it needs to be seen very clearly that a breach of Rule—technically a "fault"—is strictly amoral; thus the *cause* of a fault might be sinful, negative, or virtuous. If a man misses Mass when his Rule prescribes it, by plain downright laziness, then he has committed both a fault and a sin, but his sin is not "Rule-breaking"—there is no such thing—but sloth. If he misses Mass through oversleeping (assuming it was not a drunken stupor, which would involve gluttony) or by missing the 'bus or having a puncture; then he has made a fault but there is no sin. Or he may miss Mass because, while walking to church, he stops to rescue someone trapped in a burning house, or assists the victims of an accident. He has still made a fault, but rather than sinning, he has gained the virtue (for himself and the Church) of a positive act of charity. The Pharisee would doubtless pass by on the other side of the road and be dutifully present at Mass, but then Rule and legalism will never fit.

There are two practical reasons why all this, far from splitting hairs, is very important. Firstly, because the idea that embracing Rule is going to open up a whole new range of "sins" is apt to frighten people away from it altogether. Secondly, because Regular penitents are for ever "confessing" breaches of Rule. This is dangerous, not only because faults are not sins, but because this practice tends to cover up what might be *real* sin—the *cause* of the fault, usually sloth or pride, but possibly any other root sin. So Proficiency demands that sins and faults be clearly distinguished, and strictly confined to the Confessional and Direction respectively.

(5) *Rule is, and must always remain, variable.* The idea persists that once you have embraced Rule you must "stick it out" at all costs for ever! Rule may be *relaxed*, as for example during holidays or in sickness, or it may be *modified*, if say, work or charitable duties become temporarily overwhelming. The obvious but important point is that during such relaxation or modification, the "Regular status" remains unimpaired. In fact many Rules themselves embody a clause relating to relaxation and modification. There seems to me to be a practical, pastoral distinction—a proficient distinction—between a Regular, however slight his Rule, and merely a devout soul who goes to church very often and says a great many prayers. And, although difficult to justify by doctrine, there seems to be far less distinction between two Regulars irrespective of the content of their Rules. It is the difference between unreliable brilliance and stolidity, between fickleness and stamina.

Rule is also variable—necessarily so—according to our progress through life, and it will probably need revision every two or three years, as we advance or as our circumstances change. It is important to remember that the whole content of Rule does not necessarily increase or diminish in strict proportion with the soul's progress or regress. Because a spiritual director advises, for example, that the time spent in private prayer should be reduced, it does not mean that the soul is "losing ground". But more will be said of this in the section on "Periodicity". We must never lose sight of the absolute dogma that Rule is a utilitarian device.

II

We must now try to employ these principles in the construction of a good personal Rule:

(1) It is most desirable that a private Rule should be made in consultation with a spiritual director. Rule is of essentially corporate significance, and I very much doubt if, according

to Catholic tradition, a person who lived to his own Rule alone and without anyone else knowing anything about it would really be entitled to the designation "Regular". It would certainly be very difficult unless someone at least knew about it and the matter was occasionally discussed. But if a director is used, the points now to be considered are still relevant, because although he can help and guide, much will depend on personal circumstances, temperament, gifts and lack of gifts. In practice it is much better for a man to say "here is a Rule that seems to be theologically sound, and suitable for me; is it all right?" than simply "please give me a Rule". This should become clearer as we proceed. In the very early stages it is also necessary to experiment, to alter and adapt slightly, over a period of a few weeks, until the details sort themselves out and "fit" into the framework of personality and practical life. This is one of the reasons behind "postulancy" and "noviciate"—the idea of a trial period before finally settling down to the job. Here a director can be of much help; this trial period should not be unduly long, and without him it is possible to dither about for months without really settling down at all!

(2) *Rule should be, or should soon become, unobtrusive.* It should "fit", the soul should "grow into it", so that by habitual use prayer in its fullness becomes a solidly established part of life and personality. And this is the real meaning of the word Regular: a Christian who has no need to worry over much about duty, or about what he ought to do next, because an orderly integrated prayer-life has become part of himself. The daily routine of trains, office hours, mealtimes and so on, would look unbearably complicated if you wrote it all down and considered it as grim duty. A written description of how you should play a golf stroke—or for that matter how you should say Mass—looks impossibly complicated, but with practice it soon sorts itself out into an almost subconscious rhythm. We are forced to tabulate and discuss Rule, but the same thing applies; it is much simpler and unobtrusive in practice than it is in words, and even in words it is much less involved than golf. After all a priest no more retires with the thought, "Oh dear, I *must* say Matins in the morning" than "Oh dear, I must wash and shave"; the thought of shaving

day after day for the rest of one's life is horrifying, but we do not think so "legalistically". All these things, shaving, catching the train, Matins and meditation, just get done by Rule; sometimes they are done well, sometimes badly, comfortably or painfully, with fervour or with boredom: but they are not allowed to become *obtrusive*. Therefore:

(3) *A Personal Rule should be as simple as is compatible with efficiency.* On page 21 the Rule of the Church (and basically there is no other) is set out in three columns, and this constitutes a single Rule in successive stages of elaboration. Thus column B is but column A in a little more detail, and C is a further elaboration of A and B. The art of composing formal Rule is to omit as much detail as possible while assuring that nothing is left out of one's actual prayer life. In other words, *all* thirteen items of this table normally come into a balanced, healthy prayer-life, but they need not all formally be embodied in Rule.

Much will depend on personality and temperament, and this is why Rule should be, ideally, a mutual arrangement between the person concerned and a director. Supposing, for example, it was decided to communicate twice a week, to say an Office every morning, and spend half an hour a day in private prayer. That is a very simple Rule—based solely on our column A—and to my mind it is a very good one; in a great many cases it would be unnecessary to go any further. But it might so happen that the soul in question was a bit lazy about mental prayer, and not very good at it. Conversely he might be so absorbed by meditation that he never has any time for petition or thanksgiving. In these cases it might be sensible to elaborate just enough to ensure that nothing fundamental gets left out altogether; the initial 30 minutes of private prayer could be split up into 10 for mental prayer and 20 for the rest, in the former case; and 20 and 10 in the latter. Or the first soul could set aside one day a week for mental prayer, and the second a day a week for colloquy.

On the other hand, if a Rule provided for, say, two hours a week of general colloquy, it would be pretty difficult *not* to include all the items in column C, so there would be no point in meticulously splitting up the time into five periods of 24 minutes each: unless you have the sort of temperament that enjoys that kind of ultra-orderliness! The ramifications are infinite, and if it still looks hopelessly complicated—I do not really think it should—remember that you need only worry about your *own* Rule, not those of other people. It is only a matter of common principle and common sense.

As I have suggested before, and it is only a suggestion with which others may disagree, I think it is unpractical, or at least more trouble than it is worth, to embody the *details* of fasting and almsgiving into formal Rule. These are ordinary Christian duties and it is well to recognize obligation with regard to them, even to plan and budget for them, but within Rule I think it would be rather petty to regard a ham sandwich on Friday as a "fault". And as we shall see in the next chapter, Recollection, one of the most necessary and practical parts of Rule with which fasting is associated, cannot by its very nature be very clearly detailed.

(4) *A good personal Rule should demand creative discipline without burden.* I think this point is worthy of a separate heading, although it is very near to (2) above. Quite simply Rule should be neither too difficult nor too easy. But here temperament should be considered: some people seem to make most progress by aiming very high and continually falling just short; by embracing a Rule that is so difficult that it is almost impossible to keep without fault. On the other hand there are those who prefer to use Rule as a minimum below which they seldom fall and frequently exceed. There is no accounting for tastes! Although legitimate in certain cases, there are very obvious dangers in both these attitudes. In general, therefore, I think Rule should be such that it is invariably kept without strain but *occasionally* makes a definite demand on the will. It should normally be kept with no fault occasionally, a few faults frequently, and if it goes all to pieces very rarely there is little to worry about.

Finally we should not be afraid to modify or relax now and then, as circumstances demand, and it is preferable to relax *in advance* where possible. If next Thursday week is to be a very busy day, with several important appointments and the Old Boys' dinner in the evening, then there is not going to be much prayer, in which case it is better and more efficient to decide on relaxation at once, rather than worry all day, or just forget, and spend Friday calculating the faults. Needless to say this can be overdone, equally needless to say, a director solves the whole problem.

III

For purposes of simplicity we have been examining the basic principles of Rule in a strictly personal sense, and although a person embracing Rule in association with a spiritual director is a true Regular, this term more often applies to those living by "common" Rule. This means that a number of people embrace a basic standard Rule, variable in detail, and are thus united in a common bond of spiritual support, fellowship and love. Such a "standard" Rule is always extremely simple after the style first discussed in (III, 3) above: that confined entirely to our column A, which allows for as much variety in personal detail as is compatible with common fellowship. (I do not think I am giving away trade secrets if I mention that the standard Rule of the Oratory of the Good Shepherd adapts itself quite happily to the needs of bishops, dons, schoolmasters, parish priests, ordinands, retired clergy, and missionaries.)

The advantages of common Rule are the support, fellowship and love already mentioned, but much more important is that it gives tangible and local expression to the theological fact that there is no such thing as an isolated Christian, as strictly there is no such thing as "private" prayer. All the Baptized are one in Christ, all Christian prayer is part of the total prayer of the Body of Christ. Neither common Rule nor anything else can alter this fact, Rule certainly does nothing to create it; but it can express it in practical and pastoral form—which is of much value.

In Anglican practice, common Rule is usually embraced in one of two ways; by becoming an oblate, tertiary or companion of an established religious order or society, or by a purely parochial prayer-group or guild—there is nothing whatever to prevent half a dozen friends or parishioners from setting up common Rule among themselves.

In favour of the former it is argued that great profit ensues from being associated with a large and firmly established community of prayer. The companion of a religious order both takes and gives his share in the total spirituality of the whole; guidance is forthcoming and in times of relaxation, aridity, or sickness there is something comfortably solid and stable upon which to fall back. It is the doctrine of the Catholic Church expressed locally and tangibly. Such advantages are not lightly to be set aside; yet I think, on balance, that the more precarious parish prayer-cell or guild—or even group of friends—offers the more creative method.

The former is inclined to get little further than comforting theory. Nothing very practical is added to the mere doctrine of the unity of all in the mystical Body when one's "companions" in the companionship are dispersed over the globe; there is little practical significance in keeping common Rule with a list of names.

The latter method—the parish group—forfeits the admitted value of strength and stability, but I think this is offset by the factual expression of love, fellowship and support of those in close social proximity. And there are two further advantages of considerable importance. *All* Christianity must contain a local element. Whatever our Rule, our relations with others, or with a director; we are, by virtue of being Christians, essentially *parishioners.* If you cannot have an "isolated" Christian, nor can there be one who is not a member of, in the widest theological sense, a "parish", because that is the working unit of Christian sacramental life. "Parochialism" is a question, not merely of organization and administration, but of theology.

Secondly, with Rule on a parochial basis, much of it can be shared literally in common; certainly the Mass and possibly the Office. Once the Office is recognized as the offering of the Church, it may be of some significance to know that it is being shared by a particular list of people whose names and addresses are familiar. But to say the Office in your parish church with George from next door and Mary from over the way, is a much more creative thing.

We must not rule out the possible ideal of combining the

best of both sides. If a parish contained six or eight tertiaries or companions of the same community, we should have an arrangement as nearly perfect as one dare hope.

IV

Regulars usually make periodic reports on their general progress and their keeping of Rule. When common Rule is embraced locally this is often done orally, if this is impossible or undesirable, it is done—as in the case of private Rule—privately to a director, or by letter. This is called "chapter of faults" and although it need not necessarily constitute part of Rule itself it is a valuable practice. It is satisfying to check up occasionally as a rough guide as to how things are going—when a cricketer is out he rather naturally wants to know how many runs he scored. A common "chapter" is itself no mean strand in the total bond of fellowship, and may even act as a corporate expression of weakness and humility before God. And there is an obvious "psychological" value—in the popular not too accurate sense—in what might be called the "clean slate complex". We embrace Rule in spirit not according to the letter; too much attention to the means can endanger the end. But we must be sensible, if we never make a fault, there is something wrong with our Rule, yet there is something rather unsatisfying in allowing faults to pile up over a long period. The chapter of faults provides a fresh start—which is not so very important—but it may also provide that gentle little fillip to the will so often required in spiritual matters.

Chapters of faults provide the most valuable data in spiritual direction, particularly with regard to constructing or modifying Rule itself. The absence of all fault for example, could mean that the Rule was insufficient in content, but it could also mean undue strain and struggle; the soul could be hindered in its development by not doing enough to satisfy it or by attempting more than it should undertake. Without Rule it is often very difficult to discover this until damage has been done. A great number of faults of one type—say, lack of thanksgiving or failure with the Office—tend to bring to light important things which colour the whole of life, and which would otherwise remain dangerously hidden. "I keep on missing meditation" or "Intercession seems to get left out" is more constructive information for a director than "I do not seem to be getting on very well".

It should hardly be necessary, though perhaps expedient, to add two warnings. First, that the findings of chapters of faults take on both the value and shortcomings of statistics in general. They are useful only when wisely interpreted, and notoriously misleading if taken too literally. England's best batsman is seldom top of the averages, and frequently not in the first ten. 2,000 runs in 50 innings, average 40 means something; 100 runs in two innings average 50, means something quite different, for the man with the lower average is almost certainly the better player. Perhaps it would not overstrain the analogy to suggest that in both cases the only real criterion is the value to the team, and that nothing is worse than a selfish player playing for his average. Sometimes the game demands that we take risks, even give our wicket away for the benefit of the side as a whole: a fault may be a virtue.

Secondly, chapters of faults have no direct bearing on the Confessional, and although faults "confessed" in the sacrament of Penance are a nuisance, they do little harm. But the converse is much more serious; details of the cause of faults in common chapter could risk a violation of the seal. The two must be kept quite separate, and for this reason I think it is better to speak of "making", "reporting", or "admitting" faults but never of "confessing" them. If a soul's director is not his confessor, qualification of faults by very general excuses—like general laziness, or general lassitude—may be useful and permissible, but we must be *very* careful.

I do not know if there is any special ascetical implication behind the old proverb, but the one overriding, literal truth about technical Rule is that the exception proves its value.

6

RECOLLECTION

. . . and lo, I am with you alway, even unto the end of the world.

ST MATTHEW 28.20

PRIVATE prayer is the third part of the Rule of the Church and Recollection usually forms the third sub-heading of private prayer—as set out on page 21. So at first sight it looks as if we are starting from the wrong end, but Recollection is that which links up each part of Rule and welds all together into unity, so it can come first as well as last; rather like a "first Evensong" which ends one day and begins another. In what purposes to be a practical book, for the ordinary Christian in the world, putting it first seems to be the best arrangement.

Recollection is the "practice of the presence of God" and it is usually divided into two related types qualified by the adjectives *habitual* and *actual*; common words in the language of prayer. The first pertains to a constant state of the soul, the second is a discipline whereby momentary *acts* of prayer are made periodically throughout the working day. Plainly the latter practice tends to create the former state, and the latter—*actual* recollection—is that with which ordinary private prayer is mainly concerned. But it is worthwhile briefly explaining the former term because it has connections with other things that we must consider later.

I

The state of soul described as (habitually) recollected is the highest degree of proficiency to which we can normally hope to attain, and whatever our prayer technique and Rule, it is well to have our eyes fixed clearly on the target. This is the state of permanent God-centredness wherein the presence of God is known, felt or realized continuously and without major interruption. This knowledge or experience may be subconscious, in the ordinary practical life of busy people it will often have to be, but it is nevertheless very real and it will colour the whole of life. The recollected character is one who manifests a faith that sees God as the true end of all things, whether large or small, sorrowful or joyous, grim or gay; and he is known to his friends as someone who is balanced, level-headed or reliable, one who makes a success of life because he has things in perspective. In fact habitual recollection implies a love for God analogous to a man's love for his wife. He will "actually" think of her fairly frequently, but mostly he will get on with his work, efficiently and joyfully, for her sake. Subconsciously he never leaves her, but this does not make him inefficient at work like the love-sick youth who cannot concentrate on anything but the object of his affection. Rather this love is itself the really constant thing which inspires rather than hinders everyday work; it gives everything an object and a purpose. This is one place where the doctrine of the Church as the Bride of Christ will help us—so long as we think sensibly in terms of efficient housework as well as "devotion".

St Teresa says: "It is called recollection because the soul collects together all the faculties and enters within itself to be with its God." Now it is only too apparent that most of us are not very recollected at all, and the opposite of recollection is that perennial spiritual nuisance—distraction. But this present discussion is proved to be well worth while if only for uncovering two most useful weapons against it; the realization that distractions are inevitable and no cause for anxiety, and the practice of actual recollection. We shall deal with these in due course; meanwhile we must face up to our "habitual state of distraction", try to understand it and see how best it can be fought.

Excluding the rather outmoded word "faculties", St Teresa points to the ideal where all our thoughts, emotions, volitions, feelings, and interests are knit into a harmony because they all point Godwards; whereas experience shows us to be a mass of conflicts. When the alarum goes off early in the morning, a strong part of us really wants to get up unhurriedly and go to Mass; another part does not want to get up at all. Something tells us that duty comes before comfort and grace before nature, and another bit of nature backs this up by hinting that we shall enjoy sausages and bacon so much better when we get back; which seems subtly disconcerting and unworthy. We really are tired and we must keep up our strength, so perhaps a little more rest would be charitable towards our family and our firm. And so it goes on. It is all a jumble. But right conquers, after a fashion, and we get to Mass—a little hurriedly and without much preparation. During the Epistle we wonder if our unshaven chin is very noticeable, the Gospel is punctuated by a series of yawns, we are back in bed again for the Creed, and the bacon and sausage smell rather attractive during the offertory. We are not recollected, we are distracted. What we *should* do is to rise, shave and dress unhurriedly, walk to church in the presence of Christ alone, worship worthily, hear Mass prayerfully, communicate joyfully, and—in an Incarnational religion this is very important—enjoy sausage and bacon more than anyone has ever enjoyed it before: prayer must colour the *whole* of life, for that is what habitual recollection means. If this rather shows us up, if St Teresa's ideal seems glib and unattainable; then we are not to worry unduly, we are at least facing facts and so getting down to something practical and solid. And we may perhaps take heart from the fact that no less a man than St Paul knew the experience all too well:

"For the good that I would I do not: but the evil which I would not that I practise. . . . For I delight in the law of God after the inward man: but I see a different law in my members, warring against the law of my mind, and bringing me into captivity under the law of sin which is in my members. Oh wretched man that I am! who shall deliver me from the body of this death?"[1]

That is surely one of the most lucid descriptions of the distracted state that has ever been written, and yet:

"I thank God through Jesus Christ Our Lord . . ."

[1] Rom. 7.19–24.

Our souls, that is our selves, are like a jumbled heap of pins: interests, thoughts, emotions, volitions, and feelings—our life at work, our life of play, our domestic and social life, our life in the limelight, and our life alone—all a heap of pins pointing in all directions and getting in one another's way. But the slow approach of a magnet sorts the jumble out in a remarkable way, confusion becomes a pattern, each pin points in the same direction, and all is achieved by the focus of magnetic power. It is superfluous to add that the only magnet which can sort out all the intricacies of the human soul is God. In short the state of perfect recollection is that most characteristic expression of the work of the Holy Ghost; the creation of order out of chaos. But we can still help, we still have our own part to play.

II

Actual recollection is the formation of the habit of turning to God at regular times throughout the working day. It is a simple, momentary response to his ever-present love, a remembrance of his presence, with or without ejaculatory prayer. Phrases like "Oh God" or "Good Lord" or "Christ" may be blasphemous oaths but they may be ejaculatory prayers of recollection, and we do well to realize this, either before we condemn others for "swearing" or before convention scares us off using them properly.

It does not matter how we choose to form and exercise this habit of recollection. It will obviously depend upon, and should fit in with, the circumstances of our particular work; those whose job naturally splits itself up into periods or shifts, like schoolmasters, nurses, 'bus drivers, or policemen, might make acts of recollection at the start, or end, or both, of each period or shift. Less regularly organized work, as of the housewife, doctor, or farmer, demands some more artificial scheme like clock-time. It should be noted that traditional practices like "grace" before and after meals, and the Angelus, are essentially acts of recollection, and should be regarded as such. Less rigid and probably more spontaneous is the habit, adopted by many, of recollecting the presence of God, in petition or thanksgiving, at every "failure" and every "success" that befalls us throughout the day. And this is probably the best and most natural method of all, which is presupposed in the next section. But the actual method chosen is of little importance so long as the acts are made, say five or six times a day; and for once in a while in matters of the spirit, this is something which we may expect to produce fairly quick results. However artificial and forced the discipline of actual recollection seems at first, it very soon becomes spontaneous and tends to flow into a general awareness of God's presence. With the emphasis on practical Christian life in the world, I think this proves the wisdom of dealing with recollection before we go on to the more specific parts of private prayer. It is so easy to go to church and say our morning and evening prayers, and forget all about God in between times. Once our work-a-day life is coloured by his presence, we are not likely to forget to go to Mass, and we shall want it more—prayer will become more of a need and less of a duty.

In the tabulated Rule on page 21, it will be seen that recollection is coupled with fasting. Quite apart from the discipline and renunciation involved, it is plain that the Lenten fast acts as a reminder of Our Lord's struggle in the wilderness, and the Friday abstinence is a reminder of the Cross. And recollection, though richer in its insistence on the *presence* of God, has an obvious connection with remembrance. Two practical little points emerge from this. I do not think I shall be too severely attacked if I say that, however laudable the traditions and customs involved, our rules of fasting are a little outmoded; the instructions in the Book of Common Prayer are really rather dreadful, and I think there is a fairly general agreement about this. And of course times have changed; when "fish" meant salted herring and "meat" was prime English beef, then the difference, in terms of renunciation, really meant something. Discounting all the stories about the modern faithful who conscientiously regale themselves on lobster and Chablis every Friday, the difference between frozen mutton and fresh plaice is not very great; I would prefer the latter on *any* day! But the *recollective* value of the Friday fish still remains, and is a most useful help.

The second point is that, if the aspect of renunciation is

rather overridden by modern circumstances, the recollective value remains *even when the fast is broken*; if social and domestic arrangements make things awkward, I think we might reasonably follow St Paul's advice to the Corinthians on "idol meats" and not be over-rigid or fussy. As we discovered when we were discussing Rule, the man who broke his tobacco fast gained more in recollection (and probably in humility and love) than the Pharisee who did not. If we are going to accept a disciplined prayer-life, then may our discipline be creative and not petty. There seems little point in making a fuss about Friday's cod if we miss Mass on Ascension Day!

III

We have been speaking rather glibly about recollecting the presence of "God". And God, in our specific context, can be seen, or recollected, under three headings; as the Most Holy Trinity, as the human Presence of Jesus Christ, and as seen and known in his Church: the three Heavenly Unities over again. All of these have specific places in the recollected life, and we will look at them one by one: *Recollection of the Holy Trinity* demonstrates what I have already insisted upon; that this doctrine of God, far from being a piece of intricate academic theology, is absolutely fundamental in our ordinary religious experience.

Speaking very practically indeed, this life confronts us with two distinct types of problem; those which we can do very little about, and those which seem to depend very much—often rather too much—upon our own action and initiative. In the first case we find ourselves worrying over the threat of war, or the hydrogen bomb, or the illness of a loved one, or the outcome of some national or international emergency. More pleasantly we might inherit a fortune from an unknown relative, or we might have a miraculous escape from disaster. These experiences immediately suggest the word "Providence", we feel utterly helpless, we can do nothing about it, and our recollection naturally turns to the idea of the transcendent Fatherhood of God. Either in supplication or thanksgiving, depending on the circumstances, we fall back on our absolute dependence on "Our Father", on his providence, love and power, however remote we may feel him to be. In this case the "presence" of God may depend entirely upon intellect and will, emotionally we may be recollecting his "absence" rather than his felt presence, which, if the doctrine of transcendence is true, is a good and proper experience sometimes to undergo. The husband who "feels" the temporary absence of his wife is obviously giving expression to his love for her, and there is something wrong with our religion if it thrives only upon an unbroken experience of consolation. Psalm 22 is as true an expression of devotion as Psalm 23, or as St Bede wrote: "He will be present with us if we are heartily saddened at the thought of his absence."

Then come the problems, perhaps even harder to bear, the outcome of which seems to depend largely on our own efforts; the examination, the important interview, the investment of money, and even the freshman's trial. Now we think not so much of the over-ruling providence of the Father, but of the personal inspiration of the Holy Spirit whom we call upon to guide us through the coming ordeal. Of course these things are not mutually exclusive, in the former problems the Holy Ghost is still the Comforter, and in the latter Our Father still reigns. But very generally the type of experience dictates the stress we place on one or other Person of the undivided Trinity. This stress is found to a marked degree throughout the Psalter, and indeed throughout the whole liturgy. Compare, for example, the collect for the eighth Sunday after Trinity with that for Whitsunday:

> O God, whose never failing providence ordereth all things both in heaven and earth: We humbly beseech thee to put away from us all hurtful things, and to give us those things which be profitable for us. . . .

Here is the expression of absolute dependence, trust, and surrender to God who is transcendent. But now:

> God, who . . . didst teach the hearts of thy faithful people, by sending to them the light of thy Holy Spirit: Grant us by the same Spirit to have a right judgement in all things, and evermore to rejoice in his holy comfort. . . .

Thus protection and dependence give way to guidance and cooperation; the first collect springs to mind as we enter the operating theatre, the second as we enter the examination room.

The transcendence of the Father and the immanence of the Holy Ghost is the fundamental experience of natural religion in Christian terms. Only the mediation of the second Person of the Trinity resolves an otherwise insoluble paradox. Recollection of the Son becomes the normal expression of Christian spirituality in life, and it gives rise to the same two types of experience in terms of Christology; seeking, and yielding to, the protection of Christ who is God and the creative fellowship with Christ who is man. The recollection, that is, of Christ the conqueror and Christ the carpenter.

IV

Recollection of Christ thus leads to the very heart of Christian living, and points to the hall mark of Christian sanctity. For what is here resolved, in practice, is no less than the glorious paradox of God's unfailing providence which nevertheless allows men the dignity of free-will. Because of our Baptism we can be quite sure that we are in Christ, in the sacraments we can be certain of grace, we are raised to the plane of supernatural life, quite irrespective of our own acts and efforts. This is the "something that has happened to us", this is our free gift from God and it cannot be taken away. Yet we have not lost our personality, we are not made into machines, we still have the glorious, if sometimes disconcerting, gift of free-will. In the Incarnation heaven and earth meet, therefore all we do, be it ruling the nations or peeling potatoes, is of eternal significance. The saint is thus never despairing yet never apathetic, never anxious yet never fatalistic, he trusts in God, not in himself, yet in so doing his most menial task becomes glorious. Whatever the signs, however ominous the outlook, however black the encircling clouds, he knows that God is almighty and God will prevail, yet he lives on, ever conscious of the indwelling Spirit. He goes on calmly with his prayers and his chores, the one in the divine Christ and the other coloured by his eternal and glorified humanity.

That is the ideal expressed by perfect (habitual) recollection. But our acts of recollection of the living presence of Christ depend rather obviously on our true knowledge of himself, which in turn depends on our mental prayer. Finally we cannot isolate one aspect of the life of prayer from another—that is the burden of this book—so just assuming for a few minutes that regular recollection of Jesus Christ is the core of our Christian practice in the world, it would be best to leave its detailed discussion until the section on mental prayer.

V

Recollection in the Church is recollection not so much *of*, but *in* Christ. When Jesus said to the Eleven, ". . . lo I am with you alway, even unto the end of the world", he meant it in both personal and corporate terms. Thus we may think of an unending personal relation with the man Jesus, suggested by the Bride metaphor, and we may also see ourselves literally in Christ by the Body doctrine. These words of Our Lord are both a promise and a statement of fact. If by Baptism and Communion we live *in* Christ, he can hardly be other than *with* us. So an act of recollection can either emphasize the real presence of Christ beside us, or it can form an act of recognition of our membership of the Church. I do not think it matters very much which thought is uppermost in the life of a particular soul, both should play some part, but it is important to realize—especially in times of aridity or fatigue—that recognition of our Church membership is as valid an act of prayer as the most vivid sense of the divine presence: as always in all prayer, fact matters more than feeling.

This takes on another practical facet when we remember that the Church to which we belong is not confined to our present world. It is threefold, by far the larger parts of it are in heaven and in paradise, yet it is one; here is another trinity in unity. Thus there is a link between the Church on earth, living in time and space, and the Church in heaven existing eternally. The Incarnation creates a sacramental union not only between spirit and matter but also, inevitably, between eternity and time. So as we learn from the Epistle to the Hebrews and from the Apocalypse, the Mass celebrated at a

6

point in space and time on earth has its link and counterpart with the eternal adoration of the Lamb by all the saints in heaven. And because the prayer of the Church is one unity which cannot be split up into "services" and the "prayers" of her members, all prayer and recollection must partake of this same time-eternal relation.

Dr Mascall puts it thus:

"The Christian has . . . a peculiar dual character. In the order of nature, he lives his own life, a life given him by God in his creation; in the order of grace, he lives with God's life, which is given him by God in his re-creation in Christ. And, the Christian life being a life in which nature, without any destruction of its own proper being, is progressively supernaturalized, the Christian is, in one sense, successively *becoming* what, in another sense, he already *is*. He increasingly makes his own the supernatural and eternal life which is the life of God. Hence on the supernatural plane he transcends the separation of past-present-and-future."[1]

The importance of this theology is that the Church's year, incorporated in the Kalendar, is of private as well as corporate significance. In practice, life in the Church, and recollection of that life, means life by the Kalendar, and we must believe that the little bit of time-space experience we call "June the twenty-ninth" really means something definite to all the saints in heaven and to St Peter in particular. The Office and Mass on that day, and therefore our private prayer as well, are no bare memorial to one of the Apostles, but the expression of this time-eternal, earth-heaven, nature-grace, link. Dr Mascall quotes from Professor Sergius Bulgakov:

"The Church's worship is not only the commemoration, in artistic forms, of evangelical or other events concerning the Church. It is also the actualization of these facts, their re-enactment on the earth. During the service of Christmas there is not merely the memory of the birth of Christ, but truly Christ is born in a mysterious manner, just as at Easter he is resurrected. It is the same in the Transfiguration, the Entry into Jerusalem, the mystery of the Last Supper, the Passion, the burial, and Ascension of Christ, and also of all the events

[1] *Christ, the Christian and the Church*, pp. 100–1.

of the life of the Holy Virgin, from the Nativity to the Assumption. *The life of the Church, in these services, makes actual for us the mystery of the Incarnation.* Our Lord continues to live in the Church in the same form in which he was manifested once on earth and which exists for ever; and it is given to the Church to make living these sacred memories so that we should be their new witnesses and participate in them."[1]

Thus the Church's Kalendar provides not just a useful means of conducting services in an orderly way, but a practical basis for our grasping eternity in our earthly lives, and it has obvious connections with the true practice of actual recollection. In fact I think most of us do look upon Christmas Day in the kind of way Professor Bulgakov teaches, but the principle can and should be extended throughout every day of the year—every feria has its eternal counterpart. We should look on each Saint's Day with as much joy as we look on our birthday or wedding anniversary. And, of special significance here, we should begin every day with clear knowledge of what it is in the whole threefold Church, especially as recollective prayer in times of holiday or relaxation of Rule. It may seem a bit strange to decide to spend the Friday after the fifth Sunday after Trinity on the beach with the children, but it is a most real aid in the colouring of our whole life with the tints of the eternal presence of Christ. And here is a most valuable hint on the gentle art of breaking Rule, the "technique of not going to Church": *never* miss going to Mass on "Sunday"—if something goes wrong, or in cases of illness, we must try to be conscious that we are missing, not Sunday, but Trinity X, or Lent II, or Epiphany IV or whatever it is.

VI

Two further aspects of recollection demand a bare mention. If we take seriously our membership of the three-fold Church, our natural-supernatural, and time-eternal status, and if we try to express these facts and not merely "believe" them; then the whole tradition of *patronage* takes on a newer, fresher meaning. A church's dedication is, like the Kalendar,

[1] *Christ, the Christian and the Church*, p. 117, and see also my *Pastoral Theology: a Reorientation*, pp. 239–42.

far more than a device of convenience; the saints have a real connection with parishes, colleges and schools dedicated to them, and if the conclusions of the last section are true, then a Patronal Festival takes on the same eternal significance as any other Christian feast. And it is the same with our personal patrons; having been born into the world on St Martin's Day, and appropriately Baptized into his name, I have no doubt at all that his intercession for me is a real and personal part of my life. In reading and prayer we develop attachments and friendship with the saints who particularly help and inspire us, which are every bit as real as any worldly association. In short; we believe in the *communion*, not the mere commemoration, of saints, thence *Invocation* of them is a real and personal part of Christian recollection. And here the doctrine of the heavenly hosts is of obvious interest—guardian angels are also "real" things.

The second point is that I rather feel, as I have said elsewhere, that there is a special pastoral and evangelistic aspect of recollection *in place*; a walk through the streets of our parish, consciously in and with Christ, seems to have a pervasive effect upon the whole. There can be no doubt that a place, be it home, shop or chapel, where prayer is constantly offered, takes on a pronounced spiritual "atmosphere"; and we are called to the work of Christ which offers redemption to all things—places as well as persons. By recollection the whole parish could become a sanctuary.

7

MENTAL PRAYER

They never taste who always drink;
They always talk, who never think.
MATTHEW PRIOR

WHEN I was about seven years old—if I may be permitted so personal a story—I bluntly refused to say my prayers because I did not see the point of talking to someone I did not know. Without condoning such disobedience to a dear and worried mother, I still maintain that that was an extremely sensible stand to make. We all feel rather foolish when the telephone breaks down and we find we have been having a long talk to nobody at all. And if we need a temporary loan we do not normally stand in the middle of the street and shout, "Who will lend me ten pounds?" Instead we make an appointment, walk round to the bank, seek the manager, and, having got comfortably settled in his private sanctum, start to explain the matter. To be a little pedantic, "mental prayer" is strictly not prayer at all, but a spiritual exercise by which we are introduced to God preliminary to prayer. If petition is the request to the bank manager, mental prayer is the preliminary arrangements that lead up to it: the introduction, the appointment and the walk round to the bank. It should be obvious that both logically and psychologically, mental prayer must precede "saying prayers". The current idea that mental prayer is something rather special, difficult and isolated from colloquy, is just nonsense. We cannot hold a conversation with anyone without an initial introduction, and as we shall see in the next chapter, colloquy with God is essentially a conversation and not a monologue.

This introduction may take many forms and it can be

achieved in many ways. It can begin with an intellectual idea of God, or with a simple imagined picture of the person of Christ. We may see Christ with the eyes of faith in the Blessed Sacrament, we may achieve a recollected sense of the presence of the Holy Spirit, or we can plod tediously through some elaborate "method"—or even use such a method with no tedium at all; it is a very personal matter. Mental prayer is thus a generic term for all the manifold ways and means of forming this initial introduction to God—it can even include spiritual reading—and it is therefore a better general term than "meditation", which, though much the same, has come to be associated more and more with the specific "three-point" method. In any case the choice of ways and means is a matter of individuality and temperament, to be decided by experiment and spiritual direction. The value of all the various methods and systems is purely utilitarian. So it is not my purpose to expound all, or indeed any, of these methods in detail, that has been done often enough before, and since the proficient Christian has no use for more than one —his own—method, it is pointless to worry him with a lot of others. It would be better to discuss certain common principles and difficulties which arise in general pastoral practice.

I

A constant distraction in mental prayer is the sense of its *artificiality*, especially in those forms—the majority—which are centred on imagination. We can be quite certain that the imagination is a perfectly respectable part of our mental and psychological make-up which is linked with sense-experience and memory on the one hand and with the formation of "ideas" on the other, hence *creative* thought. Like "creative" art—King's College chapel or the Eroica symphony—mental prayer is the product of an imagination which cannot be called false or artificial; all are concerned with the expression of "truth". And we must beware of the popular misuse of this word which gives it the tint of falsehood: "he did not really see a ghost but only 'imagined' it", "the hypochondriac only 'imagines' he is ill". Imagination is wholly opposed to hallucination.

It is true that all human experience is fallible, imagination can lead us astray just as we may be deceived by the intellect, conscience or senses, but we can act on the results and suggestions of mental prayer at least as confidently as we trust our thought or our sight. And the Christian is using his imagination in mental prayer in a more valid way than the creative artist, for rather than creating out of his own mind he is but expressing an unassailable truth; the living presence of God. The imagination does nothing to make God present, it merely assures us that he is. Moreover, the practical results of mental prayer are to be interpreted in the light of Christian doctrine, which provides a double safeguard, and as the Curé d'Ars and St Catherine of Siena discovered, it is the surest way of learning and understanding it.

What we have learned in the last chapter, about the practical meaning of the three-fold Church, of the time-eternal relation, and the Kalendar, should save us worrying about a mere "digging up the past" in mental prayer. If Christmas Day really *is* Christmas Day and not a bare memorial of something that happened long ago, then our meeting with Christ in prayer is a present fact and not just a bit of historical romance.

This is a big subject, and for present purposes I would state quite firmly that the modern Proficient can use mental prayer with full confidence in its validity and truth. It has nothing whatever to do with "auto-suggestion" or hallucination; and I would advise him, humbly yet boldly, to take my word for it. If he cannot do so, and is of a philosophical turn of mind, I can only refer him to my *Pastoral Theology*, where the whole subject is discussed with much detail, at tedious length, and with a positively abominable prolixity.[1] Or he could fall back on the established tradition of the Church.

II

The Image of the Person of Christ

Because of the unity of human personality, memory, imagination, intellect, and will cannot be divorced one from

[1] pp. 232–42.

another. A "three-point" meditation, in which we look at the Gospel story imaginatively, then intellectually, then volitionally, is only a discipline which orders but does not split them apart. We have seen that a great deal depends on the imagined picture which starts mental prayer, and we have noted that Christian doctrine is the light that must shine upon it. So when we make a mental picture of Christ, vividly alive beside or in front of us, either in mental prayer or in momentary acts of recollection, what exactly do we see? Remember that we are not inventing or creating anything but interpreting a fact; we are not bringing Christ before us, because he is there already, we are simply recognizing him. But how is he there already? If he, not "appeared" or "came", but became visible, what would he really look like—rather what *does* he really look like? And how does this appearance compare with our mental image? If, for example, we hear a male voice behind the door, we can be sure that a man is there; we may imagine a tall, fair, thin man, whereas in fact he is a short, dark, fat man. We are right about the presence of a man, but wrong about the details of his appearance. In mental prayer we primarily get to know God manifested in Christ, and we want to get to know him as well as possible; a mere shadowy "presence" is inadequate: we need to meet, in formal prayer and throughout a recollected life, the real living Person of Jesus, as he really is. We gain this knowledge by the whole process of prayer, particularly by seeing his character expressed by his words and actions in the Gospels. Here we are only concerned by his real image and, although appearances can be deceptive, we do ultimately get familiar with people by what they look like and what they say: the inner soul is expressed sacramentally, the spirit of man is interpreted through the senses. What then, is Christ really like? I suggest that in most mental prayer there are three main ideas, all valid, but nevertheless forming a progression in spiritual development.

I think most of us tend to begin with an image of Christ as conventionally depicted by medieval painters, in devotional statuettes and stained-glass windows of variable merit. By true mental prayer we enter into a perfectly real presence of

Christ in long flowing robes, light brown hair, beard, and so on. Devotionally this is quite permissible, but we are by no means tied to such an image. Doctrinally, the Son of God is eternally human and eternally divine; history need not bother us, one way or the other. But I think this conventional idea is inclined to give rise to an even more distressing sense of artificiality. However firm our faith in his promise to be with us "alway, even unto the end of the world", first-century Hebrew fashions just do not seem to fit into twentieth-century Oxford Street. A vague artificial "presence" displaces the living man.

At last we seem to have thrown off the shackles of Victorian Gothic and Pre-Raphaelite painting; do not misunderstand me, these are illustrative of our conventional but perfectly valid, meditative image. And if they help you, use them and do not worry, but beware of convention becoming stagnation. I still think that contemporary art can give a new impetus to mental prayer, for it is as much the fruit of devout imagination as its medieval or Victorian counterpart and it confounds the view, by no means dead, that ascetical theology, if not religion itself, stopped with the Middle Ages. The point is that, if it is not an irreverent phrase, there is nothing whatever to stop us "modernizing the Christ of Oxford Street". It is certainly not an irreverent practice, since the presence of Our Lord remains perfectly human, perfectly Personal, and independent of historical time. He remains "real". The more conservative among us may be a little shocked at all this; they are disturbed by Spencer's *Resurrection* and Epstein's *Madonna*, they are bewildered by Dali's *Crucifixion* and by Coventry Cathedral. But are not disturbance and bewilderment the ripe fruits of prayer? and is not something rather lacking when our meditation continues to bear no more than a shallow consolation? I still insist that there is nothing fundamentally wrong with the conventional idea, any more than there is with medieval Passion plays, but nor need we fear their contemporary counterparts in modern idiom and dress. And I think that, on the whole, the meditative image of the "modern" Jesus, alive and present with us, is an advance; this will become clearer still when we come to the real meaning of colloquy.

What has been said so far about the image of Our Lord also applies to the whole setting—the "composition of place"—in a meditation on the Gospel narrative. For similar theological reasons; the historical-eternal relation, and the universal-personal relation in Christ's humanity: the whole of his life may be lifted out of history, universalized, thence as it were re-localized. On the one hand the marriage mentioned in the second chapter of St John did in fact take place on a particular date in a squalid little Galilean village called Cana. But Christ beautifies and adorns with his eternal presence all Christian marriages at all times and places. There is no reason at all why our meditation should not be set in St John's parish hall or the Imperial hotel; or why the stilling of the storm should not be in the Thames estuary, and the Ascension from the village Green. All this tends to help our general awareness of the Divine presence in life, and it is a particular help in the achievement of habitual recollection, especially "in place". A meditation on any part of Our Lord's life, set in the town square, invariably brings it to mind whenever we actually cross that square.

So long as we keep safely within the framework of the Church's Rule; inspired by grace, absolved, guided, and disciplined by moral theology, we may allow our imagination all freedom. Our mental prayer should be bold and adventurous.

But there is a third stage in this progression. The Christ of the Gospel is, in one respect, different from his being today; rather he is the Christ of the *full* Gospel and not just those parts of it which are normally the subjects of our meditations, for the Gospel contains the Ascension. If the ultra-conventional image is insufficiently real to satisfy, then so is the "modernized" picture; because both are strictly inaccurate. The real Christ of today's life is still truly God, still truly man, but his humanity is Ascended and *Glorified*. If we can pass on to this stage, to the vivid and real presence of Christ glorified, thence outside our own limitations but still truly and completely human; then our image is more strictly in line with theology and our spiritual experience is heightened. We are lifted out of the mundane into his glorified manhood, in which we do, in fact, share. And the key to this more perfect image, either in meditation or recollection, is, I suggest, prayerful attention to this precise experience as granted to Peter, James, and John: the story of the Transfiguration.

III

Christology and mental prayer

St Teresa constantly reminds her daughters that Christianity flows not so much from doctrines about Christ or from his moral teaching, but from Christ himself. Mental prayer brings us to the heart of Christianity because it seeks to introduce us to the living Person who is the Word made flesh. We must not allow our prayer to degenerate into a theological haggle, but we must make due allowance for our frailty and weakness; we must maintain spiritual health by occasionally testing our prayer in the light of doctrine. Ultimately truth becomes part of ourselves, it is absorbed into our very life; the *Quicunque Vult* and the Chalcedonian Definition cease to be doctrine to be studied and become truth to be used and lived by. Christology becomes like the internal combustion engine and radio transmission; we cease to worry about how they work in theory as they become parts of daily life—they are just there. But the theory has to be there too, occasionally things go wrong, and we must know why they are wrong if we are to put them right. Meditation helps us thus to absorb truth, it is, ideally, an almost subconscious study in Christology; like driving a car, we are *using* science subconsciously and not merely studying it, we are just making it work. But both motor-cars and meditation need an occasional check-up or they may break down.

In the last section we have seen a progression in our approach to Christ in mental prayer, and we have noticed that the first and second type of image, though valid and useful, are only completed by the final image of Christ glorified. Let us then indulge, not in an obscure theological argument, but in a routine check-up, just to make sure that spiritual health is being maintained.

The danger inherent in the meditative image first discussed, the conventional "stained-glass window" type, is Apollinarianism; the heresy that fails to give proper emphasis to Our Lord's perfect *humanity*. And the prevalence of a misguided and somewhat anaemic piety makes this a very common failing. Fervently as we recite the Creeds, positively as we affirm that Christ is "like unto us in all things, sin except"; the central figure of our mental prayer remains obscure and shadowy, in fact a stained-glass window—cold, dead, and unmoving, without passion, feeling, appetite, or sex. Peter, James, and John, Martha and Magdalene, the bride of Cana and the woman at the well, Caiaphas, Herod, and Pilate; these are as clear and vivid as you wish, real people with real features, limbs and characters: Jesus Christ flits amongst them as an ephemeral shadow.[1] This is in fact the error I warned against at the beginning of this section; our doctrine remains academic, it is not used, carried over, and absorbed into prayer. Generally speaking—there are obvious exceptions—the conventional image of Christ is symbolic rather than pictorial, he is depicted as other-worldly, "numinous", austere and unapproachable. Of course this may be great art, it may express the truth of Our Lord's divinity with reverence and awe, even with adoration, but that is not the immediate point. Under this influence our own images are inclined to miss out humanity altogether; not unnaturally failing to reach the sublimity of an El Greco, they hardly *live* at all.

Despite the familiarity of the story, I think most of us are still slightly startled whenever we read of the healing of the blind man in John, 9.1–12: ". . . when he had thus spoken, he spat on the ground, and made clay of the spittle, and anointed his eyes with the clay. . . ." Why does this sound so strange? Doubtless the etiquette of the first-century East differs from that of the twentieth-century West, and perhaps there is some hidden medical reason for this particular method of healing, rather as we suck a wasp sting and spit out the poison. But explain it as we may, the real shock to most of us comes because we are not really prepared to face the fact that Jesus

[1] For a delightful essay on this topic, see Dorothy L. Sayers, *Unpopular Opinions*, pp. 23–8.

had all the physical organs necessary for this action; we will not admit in meditation what we know in dogma.

It is here that the "modern" Christ in modern dress and setting may help us to regain the health and perspective of true Christology absorbed in mental prayer. In fact, the very process of placing Our Lord in today's Oxford Street accuses us of that Apollinarianism we are trying to avoid. The mental process of deciding how he looks and what clothes he would wear issues an indictment of our life in his presence, even of our life in his Church. Personally, I can visualize Jesus in medieval vesture or a lounge suit, but not in gaiters, clerical black, or most other sartorial innovations that are *de rigueur* in our own culture: why? not I think because there is anything wrong or impious in such speculation, but because he does not seem really to fit into this environment, and this in turn is because he is not a *real* man.

We must never forget the ascetical axiom that the only sure test of spiritual progress is moral theology. Life in Christ, expressed by Rule, remains the most potent defence against sin, but the direct, personal, moral battle remains. The two merge as we face life in the recollected presence of Christ, while incorporated into the redemptive stream which is also Christ. But when temptations arise out of our undisciplined appetites and passions, where is the power of one who knew no such appetites and passions? Where is the point or possibility of the temptation narrative? It is plain that if we achieve anything like continuous recollection most moral problems are solved; it is not merely "Does the New Testament ethic approve of this?" but "Will Christ share it with me?", not "Dare I go?" but "Will Christ come with me?". But it must be the real Christ of the full Gospel, nothing less.

Yet do we, both in meditation and temptation, refer our problems of hunger, thirst, love, sex, impulse and passion, laughter and tears, fully and honestly to a divine personal presence who is complete *humanity*? If we do not we are forced back on to convention opposed to moral theology, or a Puritanism to which the human soul is utterly depraved, or to a Christology which makes Atonement impossible. False piety breeds spiritual anaemia.

But there is the opposite error—Arianism—inherent in the "contemporary" image. It is reputed that a schoolboy, in rebellion against some rather effeminate illustrations in a pictorial Bible, painted Our Lord in the rôle of England's centre-forward. And before raising superior eyebrows at this somewhat inadequate view, we should do well to admit that he had avoided Apollinarianism better than many of us manage to do. But he had gone too far, which is the danger of the "Oxford Street" image, and of the Passion play in modern dress and idiom. There is the risk that Jesus seen as ever-present "friend and brother" might degenerate into a religion of sentimental worldliness which leaves out Christ, divine and adorable, "equal to the Father as touching his Godhead". But I do not think it is necessary to labour this second point; those living regularly within the rhythm of the Church's liturgical cycle are unlikely to be troubled by meditative Arianism. Because of our sincere if often undisciplined devotion, unconsciously letting in a little pious prudery, the opposite error is by far the more prevalent today.

Similarly, I think Nestorianism needs but a bare mention. This is the heresy that divorces the human and divine natures in the one Person of God the Son. At the practical implication of this we have already hinted, when we were able to see Christ quite happily in sacerdotal vestments but not in any other contemporary garb; it is the danger of worshipping not Christ but his divinity in church and seeking the companionship of, again not Christ but his humanity, in the market place.

This is but a practical check on the health of our prayer, and all these dangers are diminished, if not eradicated, by the third stage of our progression. That is when we recollect the presence of the *glorified* Son; Christ, very God of very God, very man born of Mary, two natures in one Person, never separated nor confused, born, crucified and buried in history, risen, ascended and *glorified* eternally. In the practical terms of both recollection and mental prayer, the story of the Transfiguration gives us the key to the whole glorious truth; a story upon which we should meditate, over and over and over again.

IV

Intellectual Meditation

It is almost impossible to draw a line which distinguishes a (mainly) imaginative meditation leading to thought, from a (mainly) intellectual meditation assisted by image and symbol; ultimately imagination and intellect issue from a common root and cannot be divided. What is of practical importance is that we must sometimes prayerfully ponder the truths of our Faith, that they may become, not merely understood, but engrafted into our personality. In the last section we saw that truth is to be "absorbed", subconsciously made part of us, and it might be well to examine this a little more.

Compare the statements "I am an Englishman" and "Australia is a continent": both are "true", but they imply very different aspects of truth. The first is a real part of my life and being, occasionally I am reminded of it, but it continues to be a practical living truth which colours every minute of my life whether I realize it or not. But sitting here thumping away at a typewriter (incidentally, with English letters that make English words) it does not matter very much whether Australia is a continent or not; it is still true that it is, but it does not affect me.[1] Now a good deal of spiritual inefficiency arises because religious truths of the former kind are treated as if they were of the latter sort; plainly "Jesus Christ is the Son of God" and "I am Baptized" are similar to "I am an Englishman"; they are truth which positively enter into every moment, every heart beat, throughout life, but we are inclined to regard them as "mere" truth which might have something to do with next Sunday or the end of the world but are of little relevance at the moment. "You are Baptized" should imply "Of course", or at least "Good gracious", but never "How interesting". Intellectual meditation is the pondering of these truths in prayer which transforms "dogma" into living and exciting parts of ourselves. This is the idea underlying the collect for Trinity VII:

[1] Philosophers who hold the doctrine of "internal relations" would of course deny this. But that is too complicated to worry about here. I think the point is made clear enough by this example.

> LORD of all power and might, who art the author and giver of all good things: Graft in our hearts the love of thy Name, increase in us true religion, nourish us with all goodness, and of thy great mercy keep us in the same. . . .

The precise distinction between an intellectual meditation on the fact of the Incarnation and an imaginative, "pictorial" meditation on the Christmas story, is a subtlety which need not detain us. It does not much matter which we use so long as the intellectual element is not wholly excluded. What we must realize is that we all have some capacity for reasoning and it is part of our *prayer* life; "I cannot understand that, I have no 'brains'" is a too frequent excuse for what is really sloth. It is also untrue.

Choice remains free and it is largely a matter of temperament which type of mental prayer plays the greater part in the life of individual souls, but it is worth remembering that, especially in times of difficulty, the opposite method or some other method can form a refreshing and invigorating change. Moreover, to be very practical, the most potent weapon against personal anxiety is often a courageous tussle with the really big eternal truths. Worries about our Mother's illness or our chances of promotion or financial difficulty, are often seen in healthier perspective by prayerful consideration, not of those immediate things, but of attributes of God or the victory of Christ. Certainly aridity and stagnation in spiritual things are dispersed the sooner by reference to ultimate theological fact.[1]

V

Our Lady and the Saints

Personality cannot exist alone since it is developed and manifested by association with others. So it implies no disrespect or irreverence to Our Lord if we occasionally switch

[1] The common method of mental prayer in which we "recite slowly and meditate upon each word or phrase of some vocal prayer" (Guibert), obviously comes under this general heading. But I fail to see why it should be confined to "prayers", this technique is most applicable to scripture, creeds and dogmatic statements as well.

the emphasis away from him on to one of the secondary characters of the Gospel story. A meditation on, say, the Last Supper, directed at St John or St Andrew will tend rather to bring out the personality of Jesus in still sharper outline. It is the dramatist's trick of interposing minor scenes within the main plot; the rather ridiculous grave diggers, preparing for Ophelia's burial, accentuate rather than detract from the character of Hamlet. And this is particularly true of the presence of the "minor" characters of the Gospel. We learn much about Jesus by concentrating on Jairus, Zacchaeus, and Simon of Cyrene.

In the last chapter we said a little about our real communion with the Saints, and the same applies to them as to anyone else; there is not very much sense in invoking those we do not know. Again it is not irreverent—occasionally—to meditate on one of the saints, especially our patrons, in order to know them better. They will automatically widen our knowledge of Christ, and this applies very specially to Our Blessed Lady.

Some have argued that devotion to Our Lady diminishes devotion to Our Lord himself; that somehow or other she "gets in the way" of our direct approach to him. What has just been said largely disposes of this view, but we can go much further. First, those who fear "mediation" whether with reference to St Mary, the priesthood, or the Church, must logically end in deism—and they invariably do. Secondly, leaving aside the emotional and moral strength that flows from companionship with the greatest purely human creature there can ever be, it is Our Lady's place in history, heaven and the Church, that inviolably safeguards the truth of the Person of her Son. Apollinarianism and Arianism are both out of the question if Mary is Mother of God—so is deism. But again it is meditative communion with her, rather than theories and doctrines about her, which safeguard us from sins and error. We surely miss much if we forget her in those stories where Mother and Son are seen together.

VI

The use of the pictorial arts

In essence, a Christian painting is a meditative "composition of place" made permanent and significant by the artist's talent; so it is reasonable that references to art should continually crop up in discussion about prayer. Our own meditations, however poor they may seem to be, are of more intrinsic value than those of other people, yet when imagination is weak or sluggish, or in times of aridity, we may usefully take printed meditations and use them, so to speak, second-hand. The arts hold an important place in that they form a working compromise between these two methods; great painting "composes place" and stimulates, but it does not make our meditation for us. So, recognizing that no single meditation, or painting, is adequate to interpret any of the eternal truths of our faith, and using the arts more liberally than personal preferences indicate; art can play a real part in prayer—in fact looking at it might even be prayer.

The link between Christian art and ascetical theology might be worth a comprehensive study—a study which I am quite incompetent to make. But on its most ingenuous level I would suggest that Tintoretto attacks Apollinarianism, Epstein counters Arianism, and the meditative examination of both gives us something near true Christology; which perhaps Giotto and El Greco express better than either. Without making any claims as an art critic, the Madonna of Tintoretto is surely, basically, a beautiful girl and a baby; and why not? it is all rightly human. Whereas Epstein's Madonna is a prophetic study of redemption: the Virgin is strong, and doubtless some would say ugly, the child deeply symbolic of suffering divinity. Certainly our preference for one or the other gives no little insight into our ascetical temperament.

Perhaps it is not without significance here that the Church ever uses the two types of Crucifix; the naked human figure in agony stirring us to penitence and speaking of atonement, and the more symbolic figure, robed, crowned and reigning in eternal glory. Both are necessary to healthy devotion, both should be found in every Church, oratory and Christian home.

VII

One or two small points remain. Most of the classical methods of meditation conclude with the "resolution", which means that the fruits of our prayer are to be gathered up and some quite definite resolution offered to God. This tends both to combat our sins and increase recollection, and it carries prayer out into ordinary life; but I do not think I am defying the authority of the Saints by giving one warning. This teaching assumes that there are going to be some tangible fruits to gather into a definite resolution, but sometimes, probably often, there are not; in which case we are not to worry. The prime purpose of meditation remains our growing knowledge of God, it is still strictly a preparation for prayer rather than prayer itself, and there is no other test for "bad" or "good" or "successful" meditation than our general spiritual progress tested by moral theology: by the grace of God how "successful" our "bad" meditations can be!

Nevertheless, feeling and emotion have some place in prayer, and mental prayer in particular, often becomes exciting. This quest for Christ is occasionally crowned by a vivid sense of his presence, colloquy follows spontaneously and it sometimes results in a clear personal command to us. Or Our Lord may break through our meditation simply to be with us in consolation, or to instruct us prophetically. All this is the gift of God to be accepted with joy; but the big point is that, because feeling and consolation enter more largely into mental prayer than in other types of prayer, there is still no need to be distressed or discouraged by its absence. We have not "failed" because no really definite resolution emerges.

What is generally called "Prayer of Quiet"[1] is an "affective" state granted by God, wherein we simply commune with him without words or discursive thought. We need not bother with it at this stage, except to mention that an occasional act of quiet surrender to the omnipresence of God is assuredly no waste of time, especially if we are tired or

[1] Not to be confused with "Quietism" which is something quite different.

worried. Simply to kneel and wait, "doing nothing", is a discipline Our Lord can use. It is as if—to use a markedly "efficient" analogy—we are God's secretary waiting outside his office door; he might ring through, or even open the door to speak, or he might not, but it is most important that we should be there. "Blessed is that servant whom his lord, when he cometh shall find watching." And plainly this is closely linked with Rule; it is remarkable how often God chooses to speak to us when we least expect it, and terrible to contemplate how much we miss by putting feeling before regularity. And incidentally, here is complete justification for Rule formulated in terms of clock-time; however bored, dull and distracted we are, however often we look at our watch and wish the time would pass, so many minutes on our knees are never wasted.

8

COLLOQUY

Here will be an old abusing of God's patience and the King's English.

The Merry Wives of Windsor

MENTAL prayer has introduced us to Our Lord, we have sought him out, met him, to some extent got to know him. Now—and only now—can we talk with him. "Colloquy" is the best word to use for this intimate, personal, informal conversation between the soul and God because it most adequately describes the relation involved. "Vocal prayer" is too wide, since it includes all prayer in which words are used, and writers, particularly medieval writers, use it in a bewildering variety of ways; it can mean the private use of prayers in books, and it can apply to the Office, or even the Mass—none of which is colloquy. "Saying our prayers" on the other hand is too narrow, since it implies a monologue not a conversation, and colloquy is essentially a two-way relation in which Christ speaks to us as well as we to him. Both fail to give the necessary impression of informality—contained especially in the adjective "colloquial"—and both exclude the obvious possibility of mental "colloquy" with God in which thoughts are not actually put into audible words.

Personal petition is the heart of prayer as corporate adoration is its peak. It is unfortunate that Protestantism tends so to stress the value of petition—"sincere prayer from the heart"—that it obscures its ultimate consummation in the corporate worship of the Church. It is just as regrettable that a certain type of Catholicism so emphasises the Office and the Mass that it overlooks a personal religion which alone guarantees adequate participation in them. All of which argument and schism is done away once we recognize the place of both in the patterned process of the Rule of the Church. For by the "heart" of private prayer I mean, in this instance, the source of personal love which flows throughout the Mystical Body.

I

Petition

The basic principles of petition apply to all forms of colloquy and if we treat them fully we may be content with one or two comparatively minor points peculiar to the various divisions of colloquy which follow. So if this first section looks ominously long, we can take comfort from knowing that we are covering more ground than its title suggests.

The first general principle is that we must never allow ourselves to forget the Christology we have absorbed in mental prayer. Because Christ is God "unto whom all hearts be open, all desires known, and from whom no secrets are hid," we are to approach him with awe and honesty; as we are, rather than as we ought to be, or even as we would like to be—as children, sinners and supplicants. Yet because Christ is man, this approach may be honestly human, without fear, convention or artificiality. We approach him as King who happens also to be friend and father; who will use, but never abuse, his power on our behalf. Or in trinitarian terms, we may approach the majestic Father only through the humanity of the Son: strictly, Christian private prayer is impossible without Holy Communion.

The second general principle, and the practical key to the whole thing, is simple honesty; which sounds like a truism but which proves, on examination, to be an exceedingly rare quality in most of our prayer. Let it be remembered that colloquy is essentially personal and informal: it is the intercourse of intimate friendship wherein any sort of deception is quite inexcusable. Without condoning dishonesty, nobody really minds when the guest of honour at a public dinner, bored stiff, half asleep, furious at missing a boxing match and longing to get home, begins "Ladies and gentlemen, I am delighted to be here . . .". Only the most austere moralist would seriously call this "lying"; it is a convention, but it would be much more serious thus to deceive a single intimate friend. And I do not suppose God is specially angry with us when, sleepily oblivious of our sins, we join in the Mass and tell him that "the burden of them is intolerable". But we should not speak to Christ like that in private prayer—unless we really mean it. I think it would help if we make a slight but very relevant detour into the whole question of language.

Modernists plead for a revised liturgy, in modern idiom, to bring our worship "more in line with the needs of everyday life". They argue that this would give a new impetus to spirituality by freeing us from the shackles of Medievalism, convention and indeed, misrepresentation. It is urged on the other hand that liturgy is a rightly formal thing which demands a language of its own; that our approach to God should be couched in a different and more majestic idiom than that of casual conversation. I submit that the conflict is once again resolved so soon as we look at prayer as an integrated whole, rather than a host of isolable compartments. I suspect that both protagonists are thinking in terms of a solid "religious" language to be used on every disparate and distinct "religious" occasion. But once religion is widened out to embrace the whole pattern of the Church's Rule, then we may accept the best of both sides. I would agree with the more conservative view that liturgical language should be formal and distinct from that of everyday use; that we should approach God in a suitably other-worldly form. And I would agree that it is desirable for this language to be generally comprehensible to the worshipper. If Latin and Greek supply the former quality, and modern idiom the latter, then it looks as if Caroline English is the most perfect liturgical language in the world today; as indeed, I believe it is. But, and here is the real point, this language is not vaguely "religious" but definitely liturgical, and there is not the remotest reason why it should be carried over into private colloquy. I think the reforming school have a strong case when they argue that familiar conventional phrases in an archaic tongue tend to apathy and stagnation, but they are confusing the purpose of liturgy with the purpose of private prayer.

The question may be referred to Christology. A modernized liturgy would almost certainly tend to subjective emphasis; it would be directed towards people rather than towards God, and it would engender an undue familiarity with God: that would be immanental and Arian. On the other hand if Christ is truly human, he is approachable with reverent freedom; and in no case can God be deceived! The stately phrases of the liturgy inspire worship of the divinity; yet if Jesus is really man, is there any particular point in saying "Oh Lord, vouchsafe in thy goodness to succour this thy humble servant in his dire distress", when we mean "Christ help me I'm in trouble"? And is not this a cloak for what is really insincere and dishonest?

Colloquy flows from mental prayer, which is both proved and illustrated by referring back to the discussion on the image of Our Lord. The "stained-glass window" idea suggests both "Prayer Book language" and the dangers that go with it, while one would hardly say "succour", "thou", and "vouchsafe" to the Christ of Oxford Street in modern dress. The first tends towards Apollinarian symbol, the second to Arian familiarity; the sentimental "friend and brother" attitude. But all is trebly safeguarded by meditation on the glorified Christ of the Transfiguration, by the sensible private use of ancient and revered formulae like the Lord's Prayer, *Anima Christi* and the *Angelus*, and, most important of all, by fitting everything into balanced Rule.

While we are on the subject of language, it is worth noting that exactly the same principles may be applied to translations of the Scriptures. There is still no question as to which is "right" or "best"; it depends upon what you want the Bible for. It is generally agreed that our Authorized Version fits most easily into the English liturgy, and possibly that the Revised Version is better for serious study, while very modern translations add interest and fresh stimulus to meditation. What on earth is wrong with using all three?

I must make it quite clear that Caroline English in colloquy, like the "stained-glass window" image in mental prayer and recollection, is perfectly legitimate for those who prefer it. I would only point out its dangers, and insist that it is not necessary. There is nothing to stop Fellows of our ancient Universities from discussing the Test Match at breakfast in Latin, if they want to, but they do not have to just because it is the official language used on formal academic occasions.

The dangers of dishonesty in colloquy are more far-reaching still. We must face the terrifying fact that we are generally more truthful in our dealings with one another than we are with God: let us examine our more common failings by a concrete example. Supposing a man's wife is dangerously ill, his colloquy might conceivably go something like this:

> O Lord, thine handmaid my beloved wife is smitten with sickness; we humbly beseech thee to love and comfort her in this adversity, and restore her to health, if it be thy will. Vouchsafe to strengthen us both, thy sinful servants, in our affliction; that we may worthily give thee thanks in thy holy Church. Let all be done according to thy gracious word. Thy will be done.
>
> Amen.

That is a little exaggerated because I have tried, for purposes of illustration, to make as many mistakes as possible, yet it is by no means an impossible prayer and few dare claim immunity from at least some of the errors it contains. On the surface it sounds fairly devout, if a little stilted, and it needs to be examined carefully in order to discover just how bad it really is. There are, so far as I can see—though there may well be more—*eight* specific defects; and what is specially worrying, they are all to some extent related to plain dishonesty:

(1) It positively oozes Apollinarianism. Whoever—one might almost say whatever—this prayer is addressed to it is certainly not *man*, and in spite of being shallow, artificial and conventional, it presupposes neither personality nor presence.

(2) Allowing Caroline English to be at least legitimate, archaic *phrases* like "smitten with sickness" are superficial and pompous. God does not need impressing either by our poetic sensibility or by our putting on an act; this is not personal converse.

(3) Although it is right, and has Our Lord's authority, to seek him in prayer and to talk to him about personal things, it is still a little arrogant to give him detailed information! God is omniscient. Similarly we are bidden, at the right time and place, to make detailed confession of our sins, but I do not think we need continuously remind him that we are sinners; he knows that and it sounds suspiciously like mock humility. The man who is always talking about his humility is almost certainly proud. Colloquy is to be reverent but not stilted, devout yet informal; so if we are really sons and daughters of Christ, if we *are*, by no virtue of our own but by Baptism, in Christ, then why "my beloved wife"? What is wrong with "Betty"? And surely there is the best of theological reasons why the name most acceptable to God is the one with which we are incorporated into him—our "Christian" name? (how many surnames of the saints do we know?).

(4) The impersonal "we" could imply our corporate relation with the Church or it might be a literal plural—"both of us"—but it could very easily be a device to cover what is really a purely personal and possibly selfish plea. That is dishonest and stupid; God is not likely to be impressed by our wrapping up the painful truth in literary devices which make things sound better than they are. And the man has just called himself sinful! How true, yet what hypocrisy!

(5) No good purpose is served by asking God to do what he, by nature, cannot help doing. If it were possible for God to stop "loving her"—and everything else—he would not be God. What is this man really praying to?

(6) Does this man primarily want his wife cured so that they can "give thanks in thy Holy Church"? Of course not. It is flagrantly dishonest and sounds suspiciously like a bribe; you cannot make disreputable bargains with God.

These last five points all cut straight across the Christian conception of God, and they defy every point of orthodox Christology; the prayer is addressed to neither humanity nor divinity, and for good measure it is both Nestorian and Monophysite as well; certain phrases vaguely suggest God, others all the limitations of man, and the combination adds up to neither.

(7) "If it be thy will", "thy will be done"—is this really true? or are these mere saving phrases that are meant to make a self-centred plea sound a bit better on the surface? Things are not improved by this sentiment being expressed three times all rather glibly. And it is inexcusable arrogance, if not blasphemy, calmly to lift phrases from the prayer of Christ and Our Lady, and tack them on to our own private prayer without qualification or acknowledgement.

(I have a private little theory which, so far as I know, has no authority or theological justification whatsoever. Perhaps it is just a whim but I like to think that one of the reasons why Our Lady is the Queen of all the saints, is that at the Annunciation she prayed, with childlike simplicity, ". . . be it unto me according to thy word". That is absolute surrender to the will of God, and I do not believe that any other saint has *quite* achieved such sublimity since. Our Lord's surrender was complete and unbroken, but if we dare face up to the Gospel, even he found it difficult; only after the most personal colloquy with the Father, at the cost of tears and blood, did he achieve complete surrender in Gethsemane. Is it not rather dreadful to reduce the sublime phrases of Christ and his Mother to the level of meaningless devotional cliché? Of course this does not mean that we should never use the Lord's Prayer or the Angelus until we are saints, but we must try to use them reverently and honestly, we must understand what we are doing. The Liturgy we have seen is altogether different, it is, amongst other things, our share in the worship of heaven, and it points to an ideal. But colloquy is not so much concerned with ideals as facing facts.)

(8) The prayer in question is not colloquy. It is a monologue. It contains no listening, yet it is almost impossible to pray these sentiments without the Holy Ghost having a good deal to say in reply, and there is certainly nothing strange or "mystical" about this! Let us then try to rewrite it, and get rid of at least some of its more blatant objections.

O Christ, please make Betty well again, because I love her so much and my anxiety is unbearable. Help me to bear it, and help me to support her. I think my love for her

> is very real and I think you started it, but of course it is pretty selfish too. Be merciful for my sake. I ought to leave the outcome entirely in your hands and trust in your love, but I am sorry I can't. My faith is too weak and my sins stop it getting stronger; my sins, oh dear.
>
> There may be reasons why it would be best for her to die, she would be better off in Paradise; but it would be awful for me. It is my will I must ask you to do, only help me to understand the truth, support me and strengthen me to face up to whatever happens; that is about the best I can do.
>
> If she does recover—you know I really think she will—then I must do a bit more about thanksgiving—that is a resolution, please accept it; but this has shaken me up a good deal—thank you for that. Yes it really would be wonderful to kneel together at the Altar again, really before you, but it is at home I want her most; help me to see things in proper perspective.
>
> Jesus Christ, Son of God; now I really cannot do this but I am going to have a jolly good try—
>
> "Thy will not mine be done"—
>
> Oh dear, pretty hopeless, but accept it please, and supply what it lacks. All Glory to you.

That too is possibly a little exaggerated, and I certainly do not presume to set it up as a pattern; nevertheless it has certain good qualities that are worth enumerating:

(1) It is honest both in expression and content, and I do not see why it should not be prayed reverently.

(2) As we must discuss in the next chapter, real petition, irrespective of content, leads automatically into self-examination. For the Proficient Regular, petition might very nearly replace self-examination with lists and manuals and so on. We cannot face Christ squarely without consciousness of our particular sins: "*Depart* from me for I am a sinful man O Lord." It is no accident that in our pattern prayer, petition—"give us this day our daily bread"—is immediately followed by confession "and forgive us our trespasses . . .". That is an ascetical principle not fortuitous sequence.

(3) This last prayer is so obviously colloquy that it could almost be rewritten in dialogue form.[1]

(4) This second prayer is creative in that it forces us to absorb a good deal of doctrine and demands much moral effort of the will. It brings us right up against the really big things—Providence, Atonement, the three-fold Church, Christology, nature and Grace, natural and supernatural—no

[1] Giovanni Guareschi's *Don Camillo* has delighted thousands and shocked thousands more—most of whom I suspect are used to praying after the manner of my first example. I really think these books have something serious to teach us about ascetical theology. Don Camillo's "conversations with the Lord" are certainly colloquy, and his Lord is neither distant nor Apollinarian! Nor do I think he lacks in transcendent majesty. It is not for me to criticize the susceptibility of others, yet I think the real shock about these conversations is that it is exactly how most of us would pray if we had the courage really to be honest. For example:

"As he passed the high altar Don Camillo knelt down and permitted himself a discreet wink in the direction of the Lord. 'Did you hear that one?' he murmured with a joyful grin. 'One in the eye for the Godless ones!'

"'Don't talk rubbish, Don Camillo,' replied the Lord irritably. 'If they had no God, why should they come here to get their child Baptized? if Peppone's wife had boxed your ears it would only have served you right.'

"'If Peppone's wife had boxed my ears I should have taken the three of them by the scruff of their necks and . . .'

"'And what?' inquired the Lord severely.

"'Oh nothing; just a figure of speech,' Don Camillo hastened to assure him, rising to his feet.

"'Don Camillo, watch your step,' said the Lord sternly.

"'. . . but Lord,' protested Don Camillo. 'You really must bear in mind that Baptism is not a jest. Baptism is a very sacred matter. Baptism is . . .'

"'Don Camillo,' the Lord interrupted him. 'Are you attempting to teach me the nature of Baptism? Did I not invent it? I tell you that you are guilty of gross presumption.'"

There is surely something healthier there than in my first example on page 91. Compare further:

"Lord, amid so many ills this comes on top of all the rest!"

The voice answered her:

"That is how I treat my friends."

"Ah my God! That is why you have so few of them!"

But that is *not* Don Camillo—it is St Teresa of Avila!

wonder the Curé d'Ars "learned his theology on his knees"! Such prayer really is, to use a rather unfortunate word, "helpful", and it is very, very clearly, to use an even more unfortunate word, "answered".

It is sometimes argued that God does not answer prayer *literally*, but that is exactly what he always does; our difficulty is that we do not use this word anything like literally enough. If we ask a friend for five pounds and he says "certainly not", we can hardly complain that we have had no answer, and the presupposition of an affirmative in all cases does not even imply any real request. We speak with God for guidance and information, for his divine companionship, for our development and above all as the intercourse of Love. This is no argument against the practical efficacy of prayer; by the power of God it sometimes works miracles, but these are not dissimilar to consolations and experience in general: they are to be accepted with joy and thanksgiving—and regarded as good but secondary things. I still feel that "answer" is the wrong word. All prayer is answered so long as it is not made in inflexible self-will; that is, all prayer is answered if it is of the kind that God can receive, though our stubborn spiritual ears might not hear what the answer is. The better word therefore, and the better attitude, is that our prayer should be "received" or "accepted", and this is taught very clearly in the Book of Common Prayer. Here the idea of "answered" prayer is nowhere to be found, yet that prayer should be heard, or accepted or received is plainly requested in the collects for Epiphany I and II, Septuagesima, Lent III, Easter III and IV, Trinity I, III, X, XII, XXIII; amongst many others.

Practically all that has been explained in this section is admirably summed up by Heiler:

"Where the suppliant's distress yields to trust, the wish expressed in the prayer is inwardly sustained and affirmed. Yet a passionate desire does not always maintain its right in prayer. The association of the wish with the thought of God sometimes presents it in an entirely new light; it loses its absolute inner validity and is no longer upheld. The petitioner completely renounces his desire and retracts the petition to which he has given utterance, or he leaves the wish suspended, no longer insisting upon its fulfilment; his request becomes what Luther calls 'abandoned prayer'. Calvin speaks of 'waiting patiently on the Lord with suspended desires'. This, however, in no way alters the sense of solace in which the prayer dies away; in this case, too, the same psychic drama is enacted in its entirety, the struggle between hope and fear, certainty and uncertainty. The tense, painful emotion resolves itself into a mood of joy. This change of mood consists solely in the petitioner's renunciation of the absolute fulfilment of his individual wish; he regards its non-fulfilment with resolution and courage; he subordinates his will with humility and fortitude to the will of God, sustained by the confident belief that every external event serves a good and worthy purpose, determined by God, 'that', as Calvin remarks, 'even if it does not so appear, God always stands by us and in His own good time will permit us to know how little He has turned a deaf ear to the prayers which in the sight of man have seemed to remain unanswered'. Yet it is only after hard struggle that the suppliant leaves his wishes and longings with God; the natural will resists every apparent hindrance and menace, and finds no rest until the holy will of God, the challenging and constraining power of religious and moral duties and values, has disclosed itself to him."[1]

II

Intercession

The principles of colloquy discussed in the last section—its Christological basis, its meditative preparation, and the need for honesty qualified by moral doctrine—apply equally to intercession and petition. In fact these two tend to overlap and the prayers just considered could come under either heading; indeed to be quite honest, if a little cruel, it is difficult to decide whether the man in our examples was interceding for his wife or making petition for himself. In this way the word "supplication" is sometimes used as a composite

[1] *Prayer*, pp. 265–6; this whole section is of much value.

term. But intercession remains a particular part of balanced Rule which has peculiar problems of its own.

It is extremely important here, perhaps more so here than anywhere, to realize that because of our Baptismal incorporation into the One Body, hence the total unity of Christian prayer, the whole of Rule—Mass, Office and every department of private prayer—is intercessory. That is made clear by the doctrine of the Church as the channel of grace, the agent of redemption in the world, and Our Lord made it equally clear as recorded in the seventeenth chapter of St John. The practical point so often missed by prevailing individualism is that the most creative of all intercession for a personal friend is full participation in the Rule of the Church. And only by such regular participation in adoration and the sacraments of grace can there be the remotest hope that our particular pleas are somewhere near the will of God. The Mass, or even the Confessional, might be more truly intercessory than the most impassioned "intercession". The converse is tragically true as every parish priest knows so well; in sudden tragedy or bereavement the fervent prayer of the lapsed is so often "sincere", "devout", "right from the heart", and so impossibly heretical that nothing much "seems to happen". Just one Mass could do much more—and the momentary Eucharistic intention of the parish priest probably does.

But, never to be divorced from integrated Rule, a right personal element remains, and intercession may be a very special gift. In this case a soul seems to be capable of really entering into the anxiety, pain and distress of another; by prayer he can console and sometimes cure in a remarkably direct way. Like all of God's more spectacular and powerful gifts, this is something that needs careful nurture and guidance; it is a matter for specialist direction which is beyond the scope of this book. Yet it contains lessons for the rest of us, for on a quite commonplace level, suffering, especially mental suffering, can be shared, and it can surely be vicarious. The real willingness to share, almost to put oneself in the place of another, is a legitimate test for our prayer and love, and our own anxiety for a loved one, whatever self-centred aspects may enter, can be turned into creative intercession. Thus real intercession is sacrificial; we have made little progress in prayer if it never hurts. I think all that is deducible from further examination of the examples given in the last section, but intercession for a loved one is a comparatively simple matter so long as we face our own limitations—or accept our gifts—with honesty and within Rule.

A different set of problems arise as we return to the duty of intercession in terms of ordinary Christian proficiency. Between the theological fact of our common humanity in Christ, hence inter-dependence one with another in all prayer, and the intensely personal relation of man and wife; there are many degrees of acquaintance and friendship. By Rule we automatically intercede for all men,[1] by love we automatically pray for wives and children, but what of those in all the various circles of ordinary life; those we meet at work, in the club, in shops and offices, and in the congregation of our parish church? And it is plain that a man's intercession for a close friend suddenly in trouble is quite different from his prayer—however honest and sincere—for "the Church in Borneo". What is the distinction and practical technique in terms of plain efficiency? I think it would be easiest and most practical to put this question in the framework of pastoral "requests for prayer". When the secretary of a man's club tells him that "poor old Fotheringay is frightfully upset about his niece's sister-in-law being run over by a 'bus and I'm sure your prayers would be appreciated, old boy": what exactly does it mean and what exactly is a Christian Proficient supposed to do about it?

Charity demands that we do more than we invariably do, yet charity itself might involve the risk of seeming cold and unsympathetic, for we must be bold enough, in a firm but kindly way, to get such requests quite clear when they are made. Most of us are probably content with a rather embarrassed "Of course, old chap, and try not to worry", whilst the proper reply is surely "Well, I'll see what I can do if you tell me precisely what you are asking, but I'm pretty well booked up at the moment." That at least implies that we are taking the subject as seriously as it deserves, and that

[1] But see p. 100 (1).

we fully intend to do our best if we finally accede to the request.

Let us then try to bring some sort of order out of all this by gathering such requests under four main heads. In this way I think we can clarify our own duty, learn a little about intercession as such, and, if it is not overbearing pride, help others to realize exactly what they are asking, and what it all really means: the whole matter has this secondary but nevertheless valuable, evangelistic aspect.

(1) "*Please remember me in your prayers*", could mean, and I suggest literally does mean, "Please remember our association and friendship within the Body of Christ, and please do not relax your Rule at this particular time. Everyone shares in all Christian prayer but accept our personal intimacy." If the person concerned is a baptized friend whom we meet periodically, or even a business acquaintance we are not likely to forget altogether, then we have fulfilled our obligation by continuing with our Rule; possibly using this request as a spur to try to make fewer faults. In the case of a request on behalf of an unknown person, we must think a little harder; the principle explained above might still be applicable, but it might be necessary in this case to apply method (2) below. The case of an unbaptized person, or one who has lapsed, is different still; and it presents an obvious evangelistic opportunity. It may sound somewhat startling if, on a request for prayer, we immediately enquire about Baptism and Communion in relation to the soul concerned; but it does bring the whole matter into the the realm of efficiency and out of the realm of sentimentality. The various types, degrees and circumstances which can come under this single heading are infinite; the really important thing is to have the thing quite clear, to know exactly what we are promising, and how we are going to fulfil it.

(2) "*Please mention me in your prayers*" is a much more definite statement, which can only mean precisely what it says. An acceptance of this request carries the promise to mention, by name, a particular person during a formal act of prayer. But it is still not definite enough, we must ask how often, and for how long—every day for a week, or every week

for six months? It is a little disconcerting that so many ask for our prayer in a particular crisis and so few tell us when to stop! This brings us to two very practical difficulties about which the faithful are continually concerned.

First, written lists of names, societies and groups for which our prayer is asked are apt soon to become unwieldy, if not positively unmanageable. Common sense dictates periodical culling of these lists, which, if still over long, must be spread out over a period of time. But we must be firm in keeping our commitments within bounds. In prayer as in everything else we just cannot undertake more work than we can perform efficiently, and it is misguided charity to allow intercession to upset the balance of Rule; if we allow one type of prayer to crowd out another we are becoming inefficient members of the total intercessory Body, and everyone is the loser. But most of this trouble springs from the initial vagueness, for a vast amount of this type of intercession properly belongs to (1) above. And we must be firm in pointing out, over and over again if need be, that, with due respect to personal relations, Office, Mass and the total prayer of the Church remains the most powerful intercessory force there is.

The second problem arises from doubts as to the real efficacy of this type of prayer. Is the mere reading of a list of names really prayer at all? The consensus of the experience of the Church shows decisively that it is and, when undertaken corporately, the extraordinary signs frequently following remove all doubt. Theologically it has some kinship with the technique of the Office, it is essentially an act, on behalf of others, objectively offered to God, who can be relied on to do the rest. Like the Office it is, above all, efficient prayer, it is something done rather than felt, and we need have no compunction about lack of fervour or emotion in this particular type of prayer so long as the initial contract is quite clear. We are asked to "mention", not indulge in a long discursive meditation; we are given a job to do, very well let us do it, without fuss. The names can be almost "rattled off", provided, as always, that this prayer is healthily balanced by all the rest of our Rule.

(3) "*Intercede for me in my trouble*" is about the greatest

single, individual call that can be made upon us; it should be requested and undertaken most cautiously. For it means no less than a considerable period of direct intercession, for a particular person and for a particular reason, frequently repeated throughout the duration of a personal crisis. This is indeed asking a great deal, perhaps involving a wholesale re-arrangement of our Rule.

Some sort of order now appears in our intercessory life, since these first three groupings of request form a descending scale of acceptability. (1) "remember me (or someone else) in your prayers" may be made and accepted always, with meaning and sincerity, so long as we are trying to live fully within the Body of Christ. (2) "mention me in your prayers" implies intercessory lists and should be made and accepted with rather more reticence. But if we keep to the principles stated under this heading, most Regulars should be able to cope with forty or fifty names a day; even allowing for some slight recollection of each subject, that is only two or three minutes. And I do not think there are many souls—excepting those of special intercessory gifts—who can agree to (3) "intercede for me in my trouble" more than one at a time. This is a most serious business, making great demands on time and spiritual energy.

In the worthy cause of efficiency and true charity, we simply must be firm, and however much we dislike the idea, we must be prepared to refuse; any other course is being untrue to the reality and dignity of prayer itself. By refusal of course, I mean refusal of a particular type of intercession and the substitution of a less onerous type. Again it might sound a little strange but the right answer to "please intercede for my friend" may well be "I am very sorry but I am much too busy, but of course I will remember you both in my prayers." And that too would not be without evangelistic significance; let us at least make known to the world that we are taking our work seriously.

It is demonstrated once more that without Rule the position becomes impossible, and without direction very much more difficult.

(4) "*Please pray for me*" is in a different class altogether,

or rather, because of its ambiguity it might be reducible to any of the classes just discussed. But it might be a directly vicarious request. In sickness or aridity it could mean please pray, literally, *for* me, that is *instead* of me, or please say *my* prayers for me. This could be fulfilled in a wide variety of ways, and it is best to be quite clear about it; it could imply an extra Mass for—instead of—the person concerned, or a special intention at Mass, or a particular intercessory colloquy, or it could simply mean the continuance of personal Rule vicariously understood.

This account of general pastoral intercession is by no means exhaustive; there remain many cases of overlapping types, and an infinite variety of subtle shades of meaning in requests themselves. The big fact is that Rule helps us to bring some sort of order out of current confusion. We must find out, in every case, exactly what our job is, and we must make a firm stand against the idea of prayer as a nice little convention tacitly assumed to mean nothing very much.

III

Thanksgiving

Like most single aspects of prayer, thanksgiving can be qualified by the familiar adjectives *actual* and *habitual*; the first meaning regular, definite acts, and the second defining that ideal state of soul when thanksgiving is spontaneous and continuous. Plainly the one develops into the other, but it is convenient to treat them separately.

Ingenuous as it may sound regular periods of counting our blessings in thanksgiving to God is an indispensable item in any prayer life. And it is something which people find immensely difficult. It is curious that while few Christians allow a day to pass without some kind of petition, intercession and confession; a regular evaluation of their virtues and successes, which are pure gifts of God, is so frequently omitted. I think there are four main reasons for this:

(1) We do not think *widely* enough. What is really remarkable about this world is the extraordinary amount of real tragedy that fails to happen; and of course the vast amount

that does happen but not to us—which links thanksgiving with intercession on a wide scale.[1] We do not want to become neurotically fearful, but a little serious meditation on the fact that we are not punished anything like enough, is unlikely to do us any great harm.

(2) We think too little of *the really great facts.* Christians should not be remarkable for "blowing their own trumpets", yet we must force ourselves to the quiet realization of our glorious importance as members of Christ. We must believe, without pride or hypocrisy, that all the efforts of great statesmen, industrialists, economists, poets and philosophers, are impotent without the efficient action of the One redemptive channel. As Regular Christians we are, in the best sense of the word, "important", and also in the best sense of the word "successful". We must give thanks for little local things because our Faith is sacramental, but they only mean so much because of the big eternal facts: Incarnation, Atonement, Ascension, the Church. We can never exhaust our wonder and joy in the face of them. The general Thanksgiving is not prayed nearly enough; its riches are almost inexhaustible. But again, and of necessity, from the Universal to the personal:

(3) We are far too *Puritan.* In spite of our Catholic profession, our denial of Apollinarianism—in theory—and our claim to be "broad-minded", we still suffer from the delusion that there is something slightly irreligious about personal pleasure. We happily thank God for our creation and preservation, even for the stellar system and the facts of astronomy, but we are inclined to jib at all the blessings of this life. We might thank God for the sunshine and the flowers, but not for beer and dance music. Why not? With Mr G. K. Chesterton, I cannot subscribe to the view that "God made all the enjoyable things especially for the benefit of the wicked." Thus:

(4) We are *dishonest, prudish,* and *Apollinarian.* It is complementary, not contradictory, to (1) and (2) above to say that we do not think narrowly enough about little things. We regard God as, if the phrase is permissible, an overbearing "high-brow", and this is a subtle mixture of Apollinarianism

[1] See St John 17.

and Puritanism. The answer remains in *honest* colloquy. If a man enjoys taking his best friend's wife out to dinner, he might just conceivably thank God for his daily bread and the beauties of friendship, but not for lobster mayonnaise and the colour of her hair: why not? God provided both so why not give him thanks? I think mainly for two very bad reasons: first because Christ is not really human and therefore rather above that sort of thing—in which case why should he bother to create them? And secondly because social convention might stir up some sort of scandal about this relationship. But while God is not the smallest bit interested in social convention or scandal, he is immensely concerned for every aspect of his Creation. There can be no reason for withholding thanks for lobsters: "like unto us in *all* things, sin except".

In the chapter on Recollection I suggested one scheme wherein we tried to think of the presence of God at every failure and success in daily life. Actual recollection of successes and pleasures leads into *habitual thanksgiving* but for reasons just given, added to human frailty, most of us find it easier to seek God, and call upon him, in sorrow rather than in joy. We are all apt to forget God in pleasure or recreation, which is one of the more reputable reasons why the Puritan distrusts them; there is just a shadow of truth in the view that if we seek God more naturally in trouble than in joy, it is safer and more conducive to prayer to be thoroughly miserable all the time. But I do not think the tenet "safety first" is in accord with tradition; paradoxically the Puritan really seeks the easy way out.

The more truly Catholic approach is one of heroism and adventure, in the greater discipline demanded by recollection in pleasure and recreation. It is here that the discussion under (4) above is especially pertinent. What is wrong with an act of recollected thanksgiving whenever we are pleased by the colour of a girl's hair? or in sharing the pleasures of a pint of beer in a quiet little pub with the perfect Humanity that understands thirst? The schoolboy who calls on God when he goes in to bat, and gives thanks to God every time he hits a boundary is more spiritually healthy than many would suppose.

Only those pleasures and recreations which we *cannot* share with Christ are themselves condemnable, so incidentally we have a very practical moral guide, much more dependable than conventional *tabu* or untrained "conscience". We may be pretty certain that any pleasure that gives rise to thanksgiving is a right and proper one, and I see no reason why our joy with Christ should be confined to quiet walks in the country.

I have mentioned the value of the liturgical year with special reference to recollection, but I suspect that, apart from specific religious duties, most Christians do rather more about fasts than they do about feasts. There must be few Christian families who do not practice some sort of abstinence on Good Friday, yet how many go out of their way to provide an extra special little dinner party on Ascension Day? Why indeed are we so bound to secularized custom which only recognizes the *feast* of the Nativity? All this is part of the virtue of habitual thanksgiving.

IV

Adoration

Adoration is the peak of all prayer because it is the only possible approach to God perfectly known. Our worship is an attempt to face facts actively, and Adoration is the most perfect expression of the fact of God; it is living in the Truth. Prayer that does not lead into Adoration—however slowly and deficiently—is inadequate. Trying to right the world without worship is like keeping accounts on the basis that two plus two equal five; it is outside the truth. Dr Mascall writes:

"We realize, therefore, the duty of worship, not by reflecting on God's goodness towards us and then trying to decide what we owe him in return, but by reflecting on what he is in the perfection of his Being and then realizing—or vainly striving to realize—what such perfection is entitled to receive. And this supreme type of worship, which is due to God and God alone, is what theology describes by the Greek word *latreia* and what we usually know as *adoration*."[1]

[1] *Christ, the Christian and the Church*, p. 159.

Strange as it may seem, the struggle to reach this height on some long distant day depends on our *knowledge* of God, which is manifested to us in Christ; so all our honest intercourse with him—even about lobsters—helps more and more to reveal the Being of God to us. Thus the simplest colloquy assists us towards Adoration. But meanwhile we must bring this ultimate of prayer into our personal colloquy as best we can; and it is here that we most need to supplement our frailty by "set prayers"—especially by the Church's great hymns of Adoration like *Gloria in excelsis* and *Te Deum.*

We have seen time and time again how all aspects of prayer merge and fit into a single glorious pattern, how simple colloquy leads on to the fullness of worship. That Our Lord is still our example is shown by a wonderful passage from Heiler's *Prayer*:

"Jesus recognizes plainly and unequivocally the inevitability of his death and Atonement: 'Except a grain of wheat fall into the earth and die, it abideth by itself alone; but if it die it beareth much fruit. He that loveth his life loseth it, and he that hateth his life in this world shall keep it unto life eternal.' The thought of death rouses in Jesus a thoroughly healthy, human fear: 'Now is my soul troubled, and what shall I say?' 'Father save me from this hour', arises to his lips. But at once he is aware of the contradiction in this prayer to the divine mission. 'But for this cause came I unto this hour.' Then he forgets every trivial fear and selfish wish; he sees only the supreme end which his sacrifice will serve, the establishment of God's kingdom, and he speaks: 'Father, Glorify Thy Name.'"[1]

In Gethsemane, Christ begins with personal petition, it is "answered"—in the negative; then, seeing his mission, he intercedes for the world he is to save; eternal truth and value flow into his mind, for which he gives thanks; and the whole surges forward to "Father, Glorify Thy Name": the end of all prayer, and all life and all being—the Adoration of God the Holy Trinity.

[1] *Prayer*, p. 267.

9

SELF-EXAMINATION AND CONFESSION

"Of course," said the Canon, "mine is a very technical job."

MARGERY ALLINGHAM: *The Tiger in the Smoke*

THERE ARE probably more little manuals about the Sacrament of Penance than about any other single item of ascetical theology. It would be superfluous to plod through such familiar ground all over again and if it is not familiar to any reader, he can get the main points of orthodox teaching from any bookshop for about a shilling. Nevertheless, in spite of this multitude of booklets, it is surprising how much really pastoral information manages to get left out. The very popularity of the subject, indicated by all these little books, together with the fact that Penance is in its own way attractive, makes it expedient to repeat the familiar warning. Penance is part of Rule which must be sensibly balanced by all the other items: it is apt to become isolated and even exaggerated. There are those who go to Confession very frequently, miss obligatory Masses quite happily, and hardly ever say an Office; they are not going to make much progress towards Christian Proficiency. We are concerned with a glorious, and essentially efficient, minor Sacrament of Grace, not with a sort of High-Church hobby.

I

Self-examination

The Christian attitude to sin comprises two paradoxes; one purely practical and one indescribably glorious. In the first place, the volitional struggle against temptation is of awful constancy, and yet the Spirit of Christ is wholly contrary to a morbid pre-occupation with sin. Rule, with its positive emphasis on progress in the attainment of virtue against a merely negative avoidance of sin, safeguards us from any such Puritan morbidity by setting aside regular periods for self-examination. In daily life we are tempted, we resist, we resist again, we are tempted again, we fall; and we forget it, pick ourselves up, and start again as if nothing had happened. We grow in penitence, we become more and more sorry for our sins, but we should not *worry* about them; anxiety is sin in itself since it doubts the love and mercy of God. Then, regularly, quietly and efficiently, we reach our time of self-examination and bravely face the facts with Our Lord. Again, Rule is seen to be liberating not burdensome. But secondly, penitence grows and deepens with greater knowledge of God, forgiveness is the personal experience of the love of Christ, and the whole issues in the supremely glorious paradox in which penitence becomes nearly synonymous with Joy: a paradox that may be experienced but never explained.

Set within Rule, therefore, self-examination is both a continuous process and a particular exercise. Life seriously within Rule eliminates culpable ignorance, thus self-examination by "conscience" alone is made adequate by Rule. "Conscience" remains fallible but Rule trains it, and we have seen how honest recollection, meditation and colloquy automatically lead into self-examination. But the Christian Proficient cannot be content with legal "adequacy", Anglican tradition looks on Confession as a complete act of homage, humility and love; it is not a legalistic haggle leading to an easy acquittal. For this reason the penitent need not be over bothered with all the subtle distinctions of moral theology, he confesses not legally nor scrupulously, but generously. It is best, therefore, to supplement the dictates of conscience guided by Rule with a modicum of moral theology to be used in the more definite periods of self-examination preceding confession. And this is made more necessary as the conventional ethics of the secular world diverge more and more from the moral doctrine of the Catholic Church.

Most of this necessary doctrine is to be found in the various manuals. I would merely recommend that one be chosen which bases its form of self-examination on the "Seven Capital Sins". This is still the most advanced and comprehensive system of moral doctrine we have. Other schemes, including lists of questions, are either inadequate or absurdly detailed; while those based on the Ten Commandments must be interpreted and adapted to the fuller Christian revelation, which all revert to the Capital Sins by an unnecessarily circuitous route. The common three-fold divisions—the lust of the flesh, the lust of the eyes, the pride of life; or duty to God, neighbour and self—may be useful on occasion, but they are only shortened forms of the same theology. A simple working knowledge of this system seems to be far the easiest and most efficient doctrine to acquire. Confessional counsel itself is the surest way of bringing theological perspective to bear on the sins of an individual, and they are the only ones he need bother about. And it must be remembered that, although instruction by a spiritual director is much the best way, there is no positive law about formal self-examination at all; given penitence, the soul may simply enter the Confessional and pour out his heart to Christ in colloquy, without form, system or writing. It is a clumsy method, and is apt to waste a lot of other people's time, but it remains "adequate".

II

Confession: private and Sacramental

Every Anglican knows that Sacramental Confession is "voluntary", or, in the rather unfortunate language of the *Catechism*, not "generally necessary to salvation". So soon as it is realized what Penance is, it is plain that it could only be "voluntary"; a sublimely glorious privilege could scarcely be "compulsory". And, while strictly accurate, the Book of Common Prayer is just a little negative, medieval and legalistic: it is thinking in terms of "adequacy" rather than progress. The Christian Proficient should be more concerned with progress towards Adoration than with merely "being saved"—though ultimately they come to the same thing. But the wording is not very impressive; it suggests the sportsman who plays just hard enough not to be dropped from the team, instead of playing as well as he possibly can. And after all, nothing is strictly "necessary to salvation" except the mercy of God.

But the Anglican must be constantly reminded that if the Sacrament of Penance is "voluntary", then nothing could be more "compulsory" than regular confession of personal sins in detail, in one way or the other. I hope I am not unduly cynical when I wonder how many objectors to the Sacrament really do perform this essential duty in private. Yet once again there seems much to be said for rejecting the "either-or" conflict in favour of a combination of both. Frequent private confession is the normal outcome of recollection, meditation, and colloquy, and we must certainly not allow enthusiasm for Penance to strip private confession of all value. We have seen that Penance can be exaggerated, it can be used out of all proportion to the rest of our prayer-life, and this can lead to some not too healthy things. But if Penance is practised, say, six or eight times a year—or less—in conjunction with, say, weekly private confession, we have a balance that avoids the dangers of sloth and laxity on the one hand, and morbidity and scruples on the other. Naturally, it is understood that the Sacraments of the Church are always available, and we are not tied to Rule in cases of emergency; despite the wisdom of a regular visit to the dentist, we do not wait for the right date to arrive in the event of agonizing toothache!

Loyalty forces us to uphold private confession, and I would not wish it otherwise, but in terms of progress and efficiency we must look at the plain advantages—some more and some less familiar—of the Sacramental method.

III

Sacramental Confession

Sacramental Confession is to be preferred, because:

(1) It is Christian. Not only does it ensure that the fundamental duty of confession is carried out regularly and adequately, but that it is done in a Christian way. It is linked

with all other sacraments—especially Baptism—and with the whole of Christian Rule. Confession of "sin" to "God" is universal, and intrinsic to every faith; private confession can very easily descend into natural religion, and be subconsciously offered to a "God" far from the Most Holy Trinity. In all things mediation through the Church is the Christian way.

(2) It is "certain" in two distinct ways. First, absolution is certain by Our Lord's promise. The essential pre-requisite for absolution is repentance, which, like most Christian virtue, is more a matter of will than of feeling. The act of going to Confession is adequate evidence of repentance because it is a positive act of will. The objective sacramental act of God makes up for any deficiency on our part—provided our intention is not flagrantly dishonest and sacrilegious. The alternative is often chronic scrupulosity coupled with an artificial and unhealthy quest for penitential emotion.

If a betrothed couple, duly baptized and faithful, solemnly made the marriage vows in the presence of witnesses at home, and duly completed legal requirements; I think a case could be made for the validity of their "Christian" marriage. But they would be doubtful, frustrated and dissatisfied; yet this is analogous to private confession. In fact the former seems rather more theological since the ministers of the sacrament of matrimony are the couple, not the priest, whereas priesthood has very definite authority to minister absolution. It seems curious that while so many good pagans want to be married in Church, so few bad Christians want to be forgiven in Church.

(3) It is also certain that it cleanses the soul from *all* sin. There is another distinction; between sins actually known and confessed and "sins" which we may not realize we have committed, or actions which we make in good faith without knowing their sinfulness. The latter type are not "mortal" or even culpable, but they are still sins and all sin detracts from spiritual progress. It is like taking poison on purpose and by accident: the first is culpable suicide, while in the second case we "could not help it and it was not our fault"—but we are just as dead. I do not really see how it is possible to eradicate the latter type of sin in private confession; in fact

private confession seems to stop at "salvation" and fails to go through to progress. The sacramental act, with the words "for these and all my other sins which I cannot now remember" or "which are unknown to me", ensures the complete cleansing of the soul. There is no reason why God should not accept a similar plea made in private, yet there is no reason why he should—he has given no promise about it as is implied in sacramental institutions.

(4) It is a positive channel of Grace, wherein the soul is not only cleansed but strengthened, and experience shows that such grace is especially effective in the continuing fight against temptation. Private confession can only *claim* to justify, not to help to sanctify.

(5) As a purposeful act of humility, Penance gives expression to the glorious paradox of penitence and Joy in Christ and in Christ's Church. Whatever our reaction to the perfect plainsong of the Cathedral choir, this is a much more "beautiful service".

(6) It provides *exactly* the right act of penance because whatever it is, it has the stamp and approval of the Church. And it can provide authoritative guidance about restitution to others for injury by our sin. Private confession can provide neither, but rather a tedious and sometimes malignant anxiety. Incalculable harm is done by well-meaning husbands and wives, betrothed couples, and close friends, "confessing" to one another, or trying to "make restitution"; instead of first getting themselves straight with God, acting on his authority, and forgetting about it: "against thee only have I sinned".

(7) It provides "counsel", which though secondary to absolution—and a poor second at that—has its value. Like direction as a whole, this saves the Christian Proficient from bothering with a great deal of theology. There is no need to plough through tomes of moral theological intricacy when any competent confessor can sort out your own confession for you—and you need not worry about any other. Even given all knowledge, no one can see clearly into himself. A fair proportion of first confessions have things hopelessly out of perspective, many worry themselves to distraction over comparatively minor faults while giving a bare mention to

sin that is, ascetically, much more serious. In early confessions a simple re-orientation in the light of moral theology can sometimes transform a life, and occasionally the cornerstone of the devil's work can be removed, bringing a good deal of other sin down with it; and the cornerstone is not usually the most prominent. On the other hand it is fearful to contemplate the spiritual state of many a devout soul, who relies entirely on partially instructed private judgement.

(8) However "private" is sacramental confession—and in a sense it is the most private thing in the world—it is nevertheless of great corporate significance. The Proficient is a member of an organism, a team used by Christ in his work of redemption. For the sake of his team-mates as well as himself he must be strong and clean; the channel of Grace which is the Church Local must not be clogged up with a lot of dirt. And however confident we might be of forgiveness gained in private confession, that confidence might not be shared by other members of the local Christian community. We may owe it to them to make sure.

This point throws a much clearer light on the "voluntary" nature of this sacrament, for both free choice and community imply responsibility, and the choice here involved must depend on far more than personal whim. As always, duty to the Church must come before private considerations; private confession can still be right in particular cases, but only when the efficient needs of the local Body have been considered. It is voluntary whether or not a cricketer consults his oculist, but if he continues to drop catches through faulty eyesight, he might at least consider the rest of the team in making his still quite "voluntary" decision.

(9) In this context, all kinds of purely psychological advantages are often discussed: "inhibitions" and "repressions" are removed by "katharsis" and so on *ad lib.* I think all this is true but of very minor importance compared with the ontological facts of the sacrament itself. So I shall be content to say that there are a great many psychological advantages pertaining to Penance, which, though minor, remain advantages. In other words, the "get it off your chest" complex is not to be scorned.

(10) Perhaps the best of all reasons in favour of sacramental Confession is "why not?". Is it not just a little silly, and flagrantly inefficient, to cut the lawn with nail scissors when God has taken the trouble to supply a very workmanlike motor mower?

IV

The emotional content of the Sacrament

I am fully aware, and completely unrepentant, that this sub-heading sounds quite shocking. It will be argued that Penance is cold, formal and strictly impersonal, and that any sort of feeling, emotion—except possibly "spiritual love"—or relation with the confessor is quite evil and out of place. There is a sense, which we shall discuss in a moment, in which all that is true. There is another sense in which it is plainly, dangerously and completely false.

It is quite absurd, and very unfair, to assume that an adolescent—or adult for that matter—goes to his first confession as emotionally undisturbed as he goes to the post office. In pastoral fact, he will be tense, worried, possibly frightened, and his mind will be seething with all sorts of genuine doubts and queries; he may give way to the wrong kind of feeling and emotions which will hinder his confession and spoil what ought to be an act of beautiful humility. Despite their prolixity, he will search all the manuals in vain; and it will only add to his frustration to read that in Penance there are no emotions, relations, or queries. It seems more pastorally plausible to try to help him than to affirm—spiritualist fashion—that his emotions and difficulties are not really there. And I think there are six main headings under which we can try to answer some of these questions. To some they may sound silly and flippant, even irreverent, but I believe they are in fact the sort of things the faithful laity really want to know about; and the job of pastoral theology is to try to help people as they *are*, not as they ought to be. In any case, as St Paul found with the Church at Corinth, we can do God great service by answering silly questions. But in most of these cases the answers remain, at bottom, theological—so perhaps the questions are not so silly after all, however:

(1) "What will the Rector really think of me when he hears all this?" Well of course it does not matter a brass farthing what he thinks, he is only the agent of God, and his duty is to serve both you and God. But for the sake of interest, he will love and respect you as a true brother in Christ, and he will welcome you as a *Penitent*; that is, as an efficient and essentially *reliable* member of the parochial organism. From the point of view of efficiency a Penitent, however serious his sins, is essentially more *reliable* than a non-Penitent, however slight his sins: after absolution, the one has *no* sins to impede the flow of his prayer and the other has *some*—it is a matter of theology. Parish priests in conclave are always talking about Penitents in relation to the spiritual state of their parishes—and it is no bad criterion so far as statistics go. Obviously the seal of secrecy prohibits mention of particular sins, but even if it did not—if we may make such an impossible assumption—these would still have no place whatever in the conversation. The important thing is for this sacrament of Grace to take place in parishes, content does not come into it. Thus the parish priest looks on the Penitent as simply a Penitent, in terms of *status*, implying reliability or maturity; the content of any particular confession is absolutely irrelevant. This sort of Penitential "status" is the personal resolution of the humility-joy: humility-"importance" paradox. Because we make this act of humility and love before God, because we are cleansed by him, we become more efficient members of the redemptive machine; God is using our influence in most unlikely places in the world. A Penitent is a very important person.

(2) "As I have been drunk four times lately, what will happen if the Vicar offers me a glass of sherry? or will he just leave me out?" or "When he knows I've robbed my employer, what are my chances as church treasurer? or will I have to resign?" A confessor cannot use knowledge gained in the confessional for any other purpose whatsoever, or to influence any decision whatsoever—even if he remembers it, which is very unlikely. To "leave you out" in the sherry party would

be a technical breach of seal by implication, so he would not do it. Nor could he, or would he wish, to act in any way about the treasurership. (I rather wish people would not ask parish priests for personal "references" because of the professional bond of secrecy in direction *outside* confession, but the Confessional itself presents no great problem: the penitent is honest, trustworthy and all the rest because he has been absolved, never mind what his confession *was*.)

(3) "But supposing the priest suggests I relinquish the treasurership by way of counsel *in* confession?" If you think it might be a wise move then resign; if you do not agree then say so. You are under no obligation to take any notice of counsel; it is subsidiary to the Sacrament and you need not even ask for it, in which case the priest does not give any, although he might have to ask questions. But all this is a very unlikely complication.

(4) "But supposing something like that is given as a penance?" It is not very likely either, but in any case you must freely *accept* a penance—by saying "yes"—or you may ask for it to be altered.

(5) "But supposing I am refused absolution?" It is very, very unlikely to happen unless you are flagrantly and obviously insincere and sacrilegious. The worst that can normally happen is for absolution to be withheld temporarily, but that is very unlikely too. In any case this would depend on some technicality and be nothing to do with the actual content of a confession: but it is all too unlikely to worry about.

(6) "Supposing I leave something out by accident, or my confession seems afterwards to have been inadequate, and I do not feel forgiven?" Your feelings cannot make the remotest bit of difference to a positive act of God, nor can any mistake the priest might make. God knows all about human error, and he does not make rash promises and fail to keep them.

(7) "There is the affair with Emily, and we are both going to tea with the Rector tomorrow, which will be a bit embarrassing. We must not break the seal, but shall we really be able to 'carry it off'?"

Well in the first place of course, you must not mention "Emily"; it must be an impersonal "girl" and the Rector will certainly be able to "carry it off"—he will probably have forgotten all about it anyway. But can you? The seal applies to the Penitent as well as to the Confessor, and if you are really in danger of violating it by embarrassment, or awkwardness or manner, then for goodness sake go to another priest and tell the Rector about it. This is a matter of temperament which is a legitimate factor in the choice of a Confessor. But do not give way to mere whim too easily; ideally Penance should be such a normal part of ordinary Christian life that this sort of difficulty should not arise. But on no account risk the seal. Always remember your parish priest is both your Father in God and—literally—your "minister", or if you like, servant. He can always be consulted, as the advertisements say, "without obligation".

V

This leads to the whole question of choice of a personal confessor. In general, the principles laid down under Direction in Chapter 4, section III, apply here, except that Confession in itself is much less complicated, and we need be much less fussy. Direction is a very close, intimate, and subtle relation, whereas confession is, basically, the formal administration of a sacramental act. But we can still look for the same three fundamental qualities: competence in moral theology, an element of "trust", and, if possible, the right kind of "attraction". But, whereas in direction the first two are essential and the third usually follows, the only absolute essential in a confessor is valid ordination. If we keep things in St Teresa's perspective, and if we do not allow ourselves to be too finicky, we shall not go very far wrong. It is still advisable to find a priest who is used to the job and generally "knows the ropes". And, all things being equal, a holy man of prayer or a religious is *not* likely to be more shockable or less understanding about sin than the gay priest who is a "bit of a lad".

Finally, the four classical qualities that make a confessor are worth a mention by way of summary; and because the four operative words—like most semi-technical words in common use—are open to misrepresentation.

Father-in-God obviously implies Love. It is practically impossible not to love Penitents because humility before Christ is such an immensely lovable thing. It is sometimes overlooked that it is "family matters" that are at stake; confessor and penitent are both on the same side—always. But a Father can sometimes be harsh, so St Bernard, on one occasion at least (23rd sermon on the Canticle) significantly changes it to "Mother"! "Learn to be not the masters, but the Mothers, of the souls entrusted to your care. Engage them to Love you more than fear you." And St Gregory does the same in *Pastoral Care* (Book II, 5).

Physician of the soul is absolutely right in this context, but I wonder if we take the analogy quite far enough? Truly a doctor heals, and delights in healing as vocation, but does he find it interesting as well? A surgeon never quite knows what he is going to discover in an operation, he may find horrible complications, and he may allow just a passing moment of sorrow for the patient, but he is not going to allow that kind of emotion to impair his efficiency. His job remains to cure if he possibly can, and is he callous if he finds the work technically absorbing? After all, most priests rather like hearing confessions, and why on earth not? Absolution is the greatest single personal gift any soul can receive, and it is supremely joyful to be God's postman who brings it. Then, amongst all the marriage returns, finance, forms in triplicate, and hack work generally, what a tremendously creative work for Christ, the Church and the world this is! And as G. K. Chesterton has pointed out, only the Confessor is given the opportunity—whatever he makes of it—of loving souls something like God loves them, as they really are and without any humbug or pretence. Lastly, moral and ascetical theology is so interesting; "'Mine is a very technical job,' said the Canon." And I suspect lay-Penitents would be glad to know about this: I would certainly prefer a doctor who was interested in his job to one who was bored stiff with it and frightened of the sight of blood.

The confessor as *Judge* is not taken anything like literally enough. One who judges is the reverse of a despot who makes decisions for or against—usually against—a prisoner; he is one who interprets an objective body of law with strict impartiality. The confessor's personal opinion about a soul or its sins is of no importance whatever; and he is much too busy working out moral theology even to form one. Following on our discussion in Chapter 4, section IV, confessors give *counsel*, not "advice".

Teacher is legitimately applied to the Confessor's job but, being awkward, I would still prefer director, guide or coach.

10

SOME AIDS AND ADVANTAGES

The good things which belong to prosperity are to be wished, but the good things which belong to adversity are to be admired.

SENECA

I

THE RULE of the Church contains all that is necessary for sanctity, but this is reminiscent of Catechism language that speaks of a minimum "necessary for salvation"; what is not strictly necessary can still be extremely useful. Balanced Rule and direction save the Proficient from a good deal of dull learning, but this does not mean that reading, either of doctrine or devotion, is anything but a wise adjunct to the spiritual life if used sensibly and according to the interests and capacities of individual souls.

Theological reading is useful in that most modern Christians are healthily concerned with reason. However loyal and, in the right "holy" sense, obedient to parish priest or director they may be, it is obviously better to be informed than ignorant, presuming that knowledge is to be applied and used. And there is never any great virtue in blind obedience. Christian prayer, thence Christian life, depends on the great eternal facts, beginning with the truest attainable conception of God; and the exercise of grappling with these ultimate problems, however little progress we seem to make, subtly adds to the quality of our prayer. It guards us from the ever present danger of a one sided "this-worldliness" and keeps things in proportion in times of trouble. Many of us—especially parish priests—would worry far less about life's practical difficulties if we thought a little more about the meaning of the word "God", or of his Incarnation in Christ; of the Atonement and the glory of the Church. Theology brings us back to the solid comfort of fact when feelings and emotions get out of hand.

Devotional reading may inspire zeal and strengthen the will in periods of laxity; the lives—and especially the autobiographies—of the Saints can inspire our dullest moods. But, without worrying with petty little rules, it is wise to keep a wary eye on balance and to put a slight curb on our natural inclinations. Too much theology tends to cold intellectualism, and too much devotion to sentimentality; it is a true maxim that the slightest coercion towards the opposite of our natural bent is a wise discipline. A little hard thinking is good for the devotionally inclined, and a little devotion comes not amiss in the life of the scholar. Many people who have "no brains for theology", or who claim no attraction for "that sentimental stuff", could find an added interest in their lives if they would only make the occasional attempt.

As in Christian life itself, both aspects become focused in the harmony of the Mass, which, itself the greatest of all devotion, contains within itself all theology. The busy layman who contents himself with a working knowledge of the Mass will finally discover that "Eucharistic" theology overflows into all other branches.

II

"*Fellowship*" is an unfortunate word which in a parochial context takes on a rather weak and artificial flavour. Parish "fellowships", like Sunday school treats and mothers' meetings, rightly or wrongly suggest an anaemic mixture of sociology, gossip and rather dull "fun". But Christian fellowship is much more than this, the greek word *koinonia* means nothing less than an extension of the full-bodied relation of love in Christ that exists in direction. It is the unifying power of the Holy Ghost which, at Pentecost, turned a collection of individuals into the organic Body of Christ.

In this section I am only concerned with the expression of this spiritual bond in ordinary intercourse, which is a considerable aid to prayer and yet one which we seem strangely reluctant to cultivate. There is indeed a natural reticence to discuss spiritual things, but coupled with English diffidence this tends to make religion an unmentionable subject even amongst the faithful. Yet there seems no real reason why Christians should not meet together, in clubs, pubs, and private houses, as naturally and amicably as golfers or anglers. Much is gained by both the bond of common interest and the semi-technical conversation involved. In any walk of life it would be surprising to assess how much we have learned by "talking shop" with friends who share our interests; how many tips about gardening, cricket, or cookery we have almost subconsciously absorbed in casual talk. Yet prayer is a much more intrinsic and "ordinary" thing than any of these; why should it not be a normal topic? Furthermore such fellowship is the natural adjunct and support of direction, which helps us to use a director wisely. When the car goes wrong and refuses to start, we usually ask help from a motorist friend before sending for the professional mechanic, and we probably learn something valuable in the process. "Good morning, Charlie, have you made any good meditations lately?" or "Hullo, Mary, now could you just help me with a little bother with intercession" sounds a little curious, but I fail to see why it should.

In the cause of true evangelism, we must surely give the general impression to the world that we are doing something important and decisive. However tedious the cricket bore at Test Match time, he at least leaves the impression that his game is something containing much more than meets the inexperienced eye. On the rare occasions when religion is openly discussed at all, it so often degenerates into a dull quibble about morals or doctrine; it is not discussed as something that one *does*, with exciting implications, techniques and schools of thought. I do not see why a friendly argument in a pub, as to the respective merits of Ignatian and Salesian methods of prayer, should be any more out of place than a similar discussion about bowling leg-theory against orthodox off-spin. In our discussion on habitual thanksgiving, I urged that the shared Good Friday cod was only completed by a special little luncheon on Ascension Day—or on any other festival. Here I venture to add that it is this (possibly extended to friends and enquirers) rather than the "parish breakfast", that could constitute the real *agape*.

III

If only for completeness it is worth placing the *liturgical seasons* under the heading of aids to prayer, although their deeper implications have been discussed with regard to the Kalendar. The one point here is that, contrary to general opinion, special provisions for Lent and Advent do not normally come into the main structure of Rule, but these seasons constitute occasions for a right variation of it. This means that, although the basic Rule remains, it may be expanded or elaborated according to strictly personal needs. Without departing from custom and tradition, we may rightly use Lent, for example, as a time of definite battle with particular problems and sins. My personal opinion therefore is that we should not worry too much about current fashions in fasting; sometimes whole parishes seem to make a kind of corporate Lenten fast of tobacco, or sugar or alcohol. This is impressive and has something to be said for it, but it is obviously going to be more or less rigorous and creative according to diverse personal habit. It seems that individuals would be better advised to make their own private fasts—preferably under direction—which attack particular failings and nurture personal qualities. Corporate spirit is nurtured and safeguarded by Rule itself, not by its variations and embellishments.

Needless to say *all* the seasons have their significance in this respect, and we must certainly not forget or minimize the festive seasons as well as the actual feasts; in Christian life Lent is completed not simply by Easter Day but by the fifty days of Eastertide. All the seasons, as we have seen, have their recollective significance; slackness in thanksgiving might be more easily overcome by a suitable Eastertide Rule rather than a Lenten one. And nothing is quite so deadening to creative progress as a monotonous sequence of "Sundays" and "weekdays".

IV

Retreat

A "retreat" is a period of about three days spent at a "retreat house" or religious community, within the framework of Office and Mass and in complete silence: a kind of intense spiritual sprint compared with the steady marathon through life. It can be made "privately", when the retreatant makes his own plan of prayer—usually with help from a spiritual director—or it can be a "conducted" retreat, made with a small group of people (normally between 12 and 20) and interspersed with addresses by a priest who is available for confession or direction if required.

There is ample literature dealing with the form, purpose and technique of retreat, much of it published by the Association for Promoting Retreats[1] which is always glad to receive enquiries and advise. But there are four extra points of special relevance here.

(1) It must be insisted most strongly that, as an aid to spiritual life, retreat has a value in its own right, and any attempt to mutilate its structure, or use it for ulterior motives, is bound to end in failure. It is essentially a period set aside from worldly worries and given to God freely and fully, yet it so happens that troubles and problems often get solved in retreat if only we forget them. The basis of the whole thing is God-centredness, surrender and absolute silence; but there is one—and so far as I know only one—important exception to this rule:

(2) The origin and structure of retreat is generally held to be the *Spiritual Exercises* of St Ignatius Loyola; to what extent we should adhere strictly to this teaching, or what variations are permissible, are subjects of debate among experienced conductors with which we need not bother. But the *Exercises* themselves, despite their objective emphasis, contain one large section of a more personal nature. What St Ignatius calls the *Election* is a detailed scheme of meditation to be applied to the few really far reaching decisions of life;

[1] At 23, Victoria Grove, London, W.8.

vocation, marriage, or matters relating to important permanent work. And I think it can be argued from the spirit and historical context of the *Exercises* that the decision to embrace Rule, or to seek regular direction, is sufficiently important and vocational to qualify. Provided a person has had reasonable experience in the ordinary ways of pastoral prayer—provided that is, that he is a reasonably "good Churchman"—retreat may be a good test, and a good start, to Regular proficiency. Furthermore:

(3) Rule is sure to seem a little artificial and onerous at the beginning; all new techniques are cumbersome until each considered detail fits into a single harmony. At first, learning to drive a car demands a seemingly impossible combination of movements by hands, feet, and eyes, which suddenly become synchronized into a single rhythm—we "get the feel" of it. Thus, while it is possible to learn to drive by a series of weekly lessons spread over several months; technique and control may be gained more quickly by two or three days continuous practice. After such intensive experiment a man may not be a very good driver, but he will have gained confidence which continuing experience will supplement. So retreat might be a good way of mastering that basic technique of living to Rule whereby it becomes an unobtrusive and natural part of ordinary life; it gives us an early desire, or "taste" for spiritual things. The considerable effort required by a three-day retreat may well taper off into a wisely constructed general Rule without burden or strain; habits of prayer can be acquired which might otherwise take months to form.

A further point is that the bond of true fellowship so often lacking in parish life is much more readily and spontaneously expressed in retreat. It is ironical that a dozen complete strangers so often gain a sense of deep spiritual interdependence in a three-day retreat which is lacking in congregations worshipping together week after week for years on end. Again the "feel" or "taste" of the thing is important, even to individuals, and retreatants, like penitents, may well exercise a deep and lasting influence on their own parishes. And, although rather wide of our context here, the significance of organized parish retreats is obvious enough.

(4) Sufferers from aridity, or spiritual dullness, are comparable with sportsmen who are "stale" or "out of form", and there are two main ways of attacking this problem. A man may give up his game for a period, have a rest from it, in the hope that he will return with fresh zeal and energy; or he can go on and on until he plays himself out of his "bad patch". So with prayer, a little holiday from it is sometimes necessary, or difficulties may be overcome by plodding on, or even by a final concentrated effort. This choice is always a difficult one, in which external direction is strongly advisable, but if the latter alternative is chosen, retreat ably fulfils the need.

V

Although Rule is best restricted to the simple foundations of Christian living, it in no way opposes the use of lesser devotional customs; the Rosary, Stations of the Cross, and extra-liturgical devotion to the Blessed Sacrament, are all proper aids to prayer if used wisely, with discernment and in proportion. But if Rule allows, or even encourages these things, it nevertheless insists on balance; little progress will be gained by daily worship at Benediction and monthly partaking in the Mass! or by continual use of the Rosary to the neglect of the Office.

Finally, "Who can look on nature and not see God?" asks St Hilary; the whole creation is an aid to prayer, and in habitual recollection all things manifest the divine presence and glory. Today's serious Christian has a not unhealthy horror of Pantheism, sentimentality, and everything associated with "nature worship", yet however abused by sin and ignorance, truth remains truth. The proficient need not fear the help offered by nature and friendship, the much despised "quiet walk in the woods with God" can be a real spiritual experience; so long as all is balanced by Rule and harnessed to moral and ascetical theology. The creation is no less good for being so frequently abused; wine does not become poison because some men get drunk.

What has been said of the arts applies to all things widely sacramental; they are given us to be used and supernaturalized, and Rule continues to dispose of worry and gives us freedom.

We may freely worship God in the flowers and the birds just in so far as we worship him in choir and at the Altar, which is the whole secret of an integrated and holy Christian life "in the world". Perhaps the most topical teaching from St Thomas Aquinas is that, while lesser men sought—and still seek—immediate knowledge of God, he was content to begin with the reality, or Being, or *ens*, of ants, stones and bits of wood. By first seeking God in creation he saw all creation in God. And this is the essential first step that many of our well-meaning Christian sociologists, economists and politicians are apt to miss; the prior question in the whole problem of the Christian's relation with the world is concerned with the ascetical significance of, and his relation with, *things*. The Christian attitude towards money, for example, depends entirely upon the Christian attitude towards the things which money buys and sells; and that is a matter of ascetical theology. The *Foundation* of *The Spiritual Exercises* of St. Ignatius Loyola contains a good deal more Christian sociology and politics than modern thought is wont to suppose.

11

SOME DIFFICULTIES AND DANGERS

Crosses are God's gifts to his friends.

THE CURÉ D'ARS

Troubles are Love's opportunity.

FR CONGREVE

THE READER need not be unduly dismayed if this chapter seems ominously long compared with the last one, for in the life of prayer the dividing line between an aid or advantage and a difficulty or danger can be very thin. Distinctions become so subtle that classification is almost arbitrary; aridity, periodicity, distractions, and even to some extent scrupulosity, are so inevitable as to become almost essential to real growth. I place these things in this chapter because they are generally unpleasant, yet unpleasant things can be, and often are, beneficial; like castor oil they are aids to health if difficult to swallow.

I

By the grace of God most of our worship and prayer is, in some measure, satisfying; private prayer in particular frequently produces pleasurable feeling. This consolation may vary from a rather dull satisfaction with duty well done to all the fervent excitement of God's loving presence vividly experienced; from little more than an easy comfort to spectacular signs of answered petition. But occasionally, especially as we advance, all this feeling and satisfaction vanishes. Worship becomes boring and worse than formal, prayer is dull and lifeless, we feel as if we have awoken from a dream, or suffered a delusion; prayer is useless and untrue, and we start seriously to doubt even the fundamental facts of the faith. Spiritual depression can be such that we begin almost to loathe religion and all connected with it. This experience is called *aridity* or "dryness", which we have likened to the staleness of a sportsman—the spiritual equivalent to a good batsman who has failed to score six times running, and who feels like giving the game up for good. It can be very frightening and indescribably painful, but like so much spiritual difficulty, the real foe is anxiety and ignorance rather than the trouble itself. So it must be clearly understood that aridity is, if not absolutely inevitable, then very common, very normal, and—most important of all—a sign of *progress.* If we examine it calmly and humbly and learn to understand it, then it loses most of its terror; what at first looks like a furious tiger turns out to be a tabby cat.

Most people mature spiritually more slowly than in other ways, and the spirituality of even an average "good Churchman" is somewhere near the moral development of a small child. Such a child, given strawberry jam for tea, will see nothing but logic in helping himself to some more from the pantry; he has to be trained to distinguish the moral subtleties involved in moderation, discipline, and ownership. And in these early stages he will probably be encouraged to correct behaviour by small rewards for obedience. It is an obvious advance when such bribes become unnecessary because ordinary morality is valued for its own sake. So in the early stages of prayer Our Lord gives us pleasant experiences—little spiritual sweetmeats—which are withdrawn as soon as we have achieved some modicum of maturity. Or, in physical terms, we learn to walk with the comfortable support of our father's arm around us, but the day comes when this is withdrawn and we have to manage alone. There may be fear and painful falls, but without these we should never walk at all, we should never learn—literally—to stand on our own feet. Prayer is much the same. Aridity is the sign of progress because we are challenged to seek spiritual things for their own sake rather than for self-indulgent ends. Aridity is a compliment bestowed on us by God who trusts us to serve him without immediate or tangible reward; to do the good and the right, to honour the proper values, without needing little bribes all the time: Thomas only believed with sensible experience, but "blessed are they who have not seen, and yet have believed".

Certain souls have lived creative spiritual lives without knowing this depressing experience, just as a few have reached old age without illness or sorrow, but it is very unusual, and spiritual directors are often more worried by its continued absence than by its occasional appearance. Proficients may, therefore, safely regard aridity as an inevitable part of their development, and refuse to be worried by it. But there are two basic factors which can be used to defeat its inherent dangers.

The first is *knowledge*. The most normal phases we all undergo during life are frightening in ignorance; even the onset of the common cold would be terrifying if we failed to recognize the symptoms for what they were. Many of us will have a cold next winter, it will be depressing and unpleasant, but we shall get over it, we shall accept it without worry, and we shall not go about anxiously waiting for the first symptoms to arrive. Aridity is much the same, and we can take it in our stride so long as we combine acceptance and understanding with a healthy refusal to be morbidly preoccupied with it.

It is the most tragic irony that so many keen young Christians are allowed to lapse just when they are making progress; they are overwhelmed by the first attack of aridity only because they know nothing about it and completely misinterpret its significance and meaning.

Coupled with this knowledge of aridity itself is a more general reference to theology. We must continue to dwell on the facts of faith and give them all primacy over feelings; God is the ground of our being whether or not we believe it, or even know of it. The Incarnation and Atonement are objective—ontological—truths quite independent of their acceptance by us or anyone else. We *are* Christian souls and ever shall be; not by our faith, fervour or belief in Creeds, but by Baptism, and grace continues to flow sacramentally whether recognized or not.[1] In the spiritual innings of life there may be many periods when we do not score many runs, but we simply cannot get out, we cannot even retire, however much we would like to. It is most important, and the one real

[1] For an admirable treatment of this point see *A Two-way Religion* by V. A. Demant.

guard, not against aridity but against its dangers, to absorb this theology during non-arid phases, especially the early ones. Whatever our knowledge and preparation, this can still be a very sore trial; we must recognize our frailty and fickleness and try to realize that if we reject now (in aridity) what we easily accepted last month, then there is no real ground for believing that the present position is the right one. During post-influenzal depression we feel that life is not worth living, everything is hopelessly out of joint, and nothing pleasant will ever happen again, yet deep down we know that this is only a pathological phase and that our emotions are, in fact, quite wrong. So we calmly, or miserably, wait until we are better and our judgements return to normal. The treatment of aridity is much the same.

The second basic factor to be used in combat with aridity is *direction*. It is common experience that if two heads are generally better than one, they are particularly so in distress; troubles are always better shared and the common bond of Christian love is a special support in difficult times. Mild anxiety borne alone can lead to serious mental disorder: so normal aridity in isolation can cause needless damage to souls.

Further, the soul in aridity is less capable than ever of making its own decisions, which—because of aridity itself—are often very difficult ones in any case. It has been seen that the proper course here might be a continued struggle with prayer in the knowledge that feelings have little bearing on efficacy and that God makes much use of our worst efforts, or it might be wise to relax and rest. Rule may need modification or adjustment, or there is the somewhat "kill or cure" method of retreat. All these constitute very delicate problems which the arid soul is rarely, if ever, capable of solving unaided.

II

At first, aridity is usually an intense experience of short duration, but as we grow in faith these periods tend to become longer and less acute; short sharp pains give way to a more continuous dull ache. Although these ups and downs continue throughout life, greater maturity gives rise to a more stable and less emotional approach to prayer. These later, more "chronic" phases and processes are distinguished by the term *periodicity.* This too, is of much pastoral importance, and again a good deal of needless distress is caused by ignorance and misunderstanding of it.

The whole life of prayer resembles courtship and marriage in that it usually begins with much emotion, excitement, and happiness, with aridity equivalent to the fierce little strains and quarrels of the early years. These are unpleasant but necessary to the working out of a stable and harmonious relation. And, as the years go by, much of the original excitement and "romance" gives way to a deeper and more constant love; the relation is more maturely satisfying and less easily upset. Like husbands and wives, proficient Christians may sometimes look back nostalgically on the pleasures of the early days of courtship and confirmation, yet they know in their hearts that the blessings of present stolidity are, on balance, the greater good.

Periodicity demands, perhaps more than anything, that the principle of Rule is interpreted correctly, for it may well be that the content of Rule will fluctuate, and probably diminish, as life goes on and circumstances change. The keen young Christian, just confirmed, may give much time to prayer and the sacraments, to serving, singing, meditation and study, and this time is available to him. All that is good, for it creates a right familiarity with spiritual things and lays a solid foundation in ascetical technique. But when the first flush of spiritual excitement wears thin, the quantity of prayer may have to be reduced, and this by both wise direction and the increasing demands of career, marriage, and family life. It is vital to keep firmly to first principles and to realize that rather less hours of prayer, or communion twice weekly instead of thrice, need not point to any general spiritual decline. The middle-aged man who kisses his wife twice a day, compared with the dozen times on their honeymoon, does not love her any less! Passion and fervour give way to steadier maturity. Through ignorance, many souls are burdened by the sense that their religious life is slowly falling to pieces when, in fact, it is but growing up naturally. But again the position can be subtle and delicate, periodicity suggests itself as an excuse for laxity; direction remains the common-sense safeguard.

III

Scrupulosity is a serious spiritual disease in which the soul is perpetually oppressed by moral quibbles exaggerated out of all proportion. The scrupulous soul is always worried, frightened, and on the verge of despair, and he will fly to his confessor and director every day—if they are silly enough to allow it. This disease is dealt with adequately in the usual textbooks, and souls who succumb to it need specialist treatment; so far as the ordinary healthy Proficient is concerned, the less said about it the better. But there is a milder, ascetical form which is associated with the corollary dangers of *Puritanism* and *tension*. The growing soul becomes scrupulous over prayer itself; each word of prayers or Office must be pronounced with meticulous care, meditation is governed by petty self-imposed regulations, and the slightest fault or distraction is believed to be mortal sin. Rule becomes Pharisaic and a Puritan grimness overshadows the whole of religion, expelling from it anything that savours of beauty, joy or humour. Prayer is indeed the most important thing there is, but the spiritually scrupulous are so overwhelmed by this fact that they are never efficiently at ease with it. Our approach to God in worship should certainly be dignified and serious, but that we may approach him freely and joyfully is the very meaning of the Incarnation and Atonement. I am not advocating laxity or carelessness, but the very word Proficiency implies quiet confidence rather than "nerves".

The good car driver is *not* the man who sits stiffly upright, gripping the steering wheel as tightly as he can, keeping to the crown of the road at a steady twenty miles an hour, with his eyes staring ahead of him in grim concentration. The good driver—and in these perilous days the safe driver—is vigilant and alert, but at the same time comfortable, confident and relaxed. So with prayer, we are to avoid the mock-pious attitude of tight-lipped gravity if we are to advance healthily. These tense souls are always talking of the pitfalls and dangers attendant on this or that prayer form, method, or approach; they are akin to the older Protestants who became so terrified of "superstition", "hypocrisy", and "idolatry" that they found themselves in danger of giving up worship altogether. But of course religion, like anything else that is powerful and adventurous, *is* dangerous, and we must set about it with both restraint and courage; we must take reasonable risks, we must indulge in devout experiment, we must trust the Holy Spirit and risk our talents rather than bury them in the sand. Christian prudence is not the policy of "safety-first". The root error here is Puritan because it can be traced, yet again, to Apollinarianism. Our Lord's earthly life was courageously *human*, it was his own personal, human decisions —"risky" ones—that led to the Passion and the Cross; each step was a decisive act of obedience, the course of his life was not "inevitable" in the sense that makes the temptation stories meaningless. This "safety-first" attitude is incompatible with fellowship with and in the humanity of Christ who knows the inmost secrets of our hearts.

Professor Farmer speaks of "value-resistance"—the necessary tension of will which arises when two virile personalities meet—and Baron von Hügel shows how such experience is rightly accentuated as we approach God. But this is the tense excitement of adoration from human to divine personality, the approach of creature to Creator, of sinner to the Sinless, of redeemed to Redeemer, of beloved to Love. It is very different from the artificial tenseness of mock-piety so often seen in the average English congregation at the average Sunday service. The parish church is, after all, Our Father's house—which means our *home*—a house of prayer indeed and not a thieves' den, but home surely implies both respect and a certain calm informality; it is an environment wherein we behave naturally and lovingly, not artificially by prescribed etiquette. To be "at home" or to feel "at home" is the antithesis of tension, which frustrates spiritual freedom. I am not of course arguing against a decent and correct performance of liturgical ceremony, any more than I am deriding decent table manners at home, but these things should be part of our lives, not the sort of ritual that goes with a military parade. We must avoid the attitude which is so concerned with conventional behaviour that it forgets all about God.

Concentration on the divine Humanity, absorption of doctrine, actual recollection, and familiarity with Rule, all help to combat this false attitude; but I think the most important thing of all is a simple recognition that tension, in this sense, is an error. Prayer is a *normal* human activity and need; religion is the ordinary life of ordinary Christians, in which gaiety, adventure, and an occasional laugh are not out of place.

IV

My remarks about understanding and knowledge in combat with aridity and periodicity apply equally to the perennial problem of *distractions*. Calm acceptance of their inevitability, gentle repulsion and perseverance, and a firm refusal to be worried, are the remedies prescribed in the usual text-books. Once all these things are regarded as the normal accompaniments to human frailty, to be accepted as "all part of the game", then the game is half won. Actual recollection, leading to a greater degree of habitual recollection, remains the long-term policy, for "what we are in our life we are in our prayer". But there are three small points—little more than hints—that may be useful in times of special difficulty.

Pastorally, I think we must treat Our Lord's injunction "be ye therefore perfect" as the ultimate, not immediate, ambition; we must aim at achieving perfect sanctity in about five hundred years time. As St Bernard said: "It is a long, long, road winding uphill all the way, yea to the very end", and this attitude is neither disobedient nor lax so long as we concentrate on slow but steady progress. We must therefore reject that tension which insists on the perfection of even single acts of prayer; we must learn to be surprised when we are not distracted rather than worried when we are, to give thanks to the Holy Ghost when our meditation seems reasonably fruitful instead of despairing when it is not. We should concentrate on steady efficiency rather than empty "devotion".

Psychologically, silence and conventional posture in church sometimes almost *suggest* distracting thoughts and feelings, especially if we give way to artificial tension so often and so regrettably associated with "our Father's house", whereas a calm turning to God in the midst of the world's bustle brings back the soul's calm and repose. The maligned "quiet walk in the fields" may reduce distraction in the sanctuary.

Or sacramentally, in the wide sense, we can take this particular bull by the horns, and as a specific exercise for a brief period, positively exaggerate tension and posture. Mind and body are closely inter-related and an almost military discipline of body and eyes sometimes helps to integrate mind and spirit. To kneel stiffly upright without support, to kneel "at attention" with eyes glued to crucifix or image, sometimes aids concentration, which is but the principle of the sentry who is mentally alert and recollected because his body is held in rigid control. And this is a mild form of the psychology behind the practice of Yoga, not to mention the common experience of everyday life; however pleasant the attempt, reading in bed or lazing in a deep arm-chair is not really conducive to mental concentration. This does not mean that meditation cannot, or should not, be carried out in these relaxed states of body, but when distraction is worse than usual, physical discipline may aid spiritual and mental harmony.

V

I have no hesitation in placing undue *preoccupation with "evangelism"* in a list of positive dangers to the life of prayer. It is good and natural to wish to share our interests and joys with others, it is right and healthy to desire to extend Christ's kingdom and to act as his agents in the redemption of all mankind. There is no greater truth than that, by progressive and proficient prayer, God's love and power subtly pervade the world around us and influence other souls. But prayer that leads to adoration remains the highest possible value, without any qualification whatsoever. All prayer is still in and of the Church, offered to God to be used in his way not our own, yet devout and advancing souls become discouraged when this influence is not visible in their own immediate circle. Those who have advanced well past the ingenuous stage of seeking directly "answered" prayers still cling to the idea that something is necessarily wrong when their spiritual efforts fail to increase the congregation in their own parishes. Not only are true values here reversed, but the subtlest Pelagianism would suggest that, whereas practical daily problems are lazily left for solution "by the Holy Spirit", the conversion of the heathen—his special prerogative—is to be achieved by our own unaided efforts.

Prayer groups, guilds, and cells are especially prone to this error. By God's grace a group of half a dozen faithful Regulars will make remarkable progress both as a group and individually, only to be thoroughly downhearted if their number remains at six for any length of time. Having defeated a dose or two of aridity and gained a measure of independence over mere feeling, they still demand of God this particular type of bribe; the adult who cannot do good work without personal compliments is little better than the child who will only obey on the promise of sweetmeats.

It is surely superfluous to add that I am not arguing against true evangelism; I am merely insisting that we keep a due sense of values, and keep all our work as Christ's Proficient workmen in order and balance. We are rightly to enjoy his good gifts when they come, and converts and spiritual children are amongst the most wonderful of them, yet if the story of St Thomas has any meaning then continuous adoration of God himself, without personal knowledge of these glorious rewards, is the most blessed of all.

VI

Religious ideas are expressed in parable, analogy, and *symbolism*. And however sophisticated we pretend to be, we think and pray in terms of heaven "above the clouds", hell "down below", the world somewhere in between, and "ladders" up which we climb or bottomless pits into which we fall. As our lives develop sacramentally the "distances" become less; heaven, hell, and the world overlap in experience and we may think in terms of good and evil, or spiritual and material, "realms", "spheres", or "dimensions". But most of us still think of God in flagrantly anthropomorphic imagery, of angels like chubby little babes with wings and of the three-fold church as a three-storey house with a "sacramental lift" joining floor to floor.

Like the use of imagination in mental prayer this occasionally worries the faithful. They suddenly realize, or half-realize, the symbolical basis of their prayer and it all seems bluntly untrue; there are the same doubts about "auto-suggestion" and "self-delusion". They feel that religion is a fantasy, a fairy tale, that it is, above all, "unscientific" and "illogical". In the main I am afraid I must offer the same alternative as in Chapter 7; I insist that "symbolism" or even "myth"—however naïve—is a perfectly reputable mental and philosophical process, symbolism is no more "false" than imagination, and I invite the Proficient Christian to take my word for it. Otherwise he must enter upon a lengthy study of the whole question of verification, epistemology, analogy, and language. But here I think we can usefully go just a little further.

In his Bampton lectures *Christian Theology and Natural Science*, Dr Mascall makes two relevant points. In the first place he attacks the old nineteenth-century "Newtonian" error of ascribing finality to any scientific theory of any age. If the phlogiston theory of combustion has given way, in the light of new knowledge, to the oxygen theory, it is because the latter is a simpler way of explaining or illustrating the present body of known facts; but this does not make the former theory "wrong" and the latter "right". Secondly, leading from this point, he refutes the assumption "that the concepts and theories of science provide the one true and literal description of the real nature of the world."[1] In other words, science consists of linguistic theories or patterns which help us to make the physical world intelligible—Dr Toulmin's "maps" and Professor Braithwaite's "models".[2]

Applied to the present problem we reach the staggering conclusion that heaven above the clouds, complete with pearly gates and streets of gold, and hell below—equally complete with fire, brimstone and little red demons with pitchforks—are more analogous to what modern scientists call "science" than is a great deal of nineteenth century literalism

[1] Ibid., pp. 7–9. [2] Ibid., pp. 61–76.

about physical phenomena. Heaven and hell, as traditionally depicted, are but the maps, models or language patterns of ascetical science; the Book of Revelation can be called either a devotional allegory or a scientific theory which aims at making heaven as intelligible as possible.

The first point implies that there is nothing whatever to stop us from thinking of heaven or the Catholic Church in terms of the *n*th dimension, or eternal space-time, or resurrected creation, or any other idea that helps us. The time may come when the Christian majority accepts a new system of symbolic representation, but it would not make the Apocalypse "wrong" and until our theological knowledge is such that this imagery is inadequate to explain it all, there is no particular reason to change. Neither the phlogiston nor the oxygen theory makes the slightest difference to the facts of combustion; the rejection of B.C. 4004 as the date of creation does not alter the fact of Creation as taught in the map, model or language pattern of Genesis.

If it is urged that the golden streets and pearly gates of heaven are not "really there", it can be argued by the second point that neutrons and electrons are not "really there" either! Admitting an analogical discontinuity between the two branches of knowledge, it can still be said in both cases that we are merely using words as symbols to try to explain what we cannot see.

The one criterion of value of all such symbolism is that it should render present knowledge as intelligible and usable as possible, and if we are to apply dogmatics to prayer, I think it would be difficult to construct a better theory than the traditional one. If we accept the theological facts behind Christ's "descent" into hell and "Ascension" into heaven—not to mention most of his own ascetical and parabolic teaching—most of the old "scientific" (which in modern terms are not scientific at all) thought patterns fail lamentably. And, as Dr Mascall points out in another book, if the doctrine of the resurrection of the body has any meaning, there is something inadequate about any "heaven" which is not some kind of supernatural "place".

So the timorous Christian may conclude that the old heaven-earth-hell pattern, and the rest of traditional symbolism, is as reputable to *use* as most "scientific" theory, and the fact that it can be so used is all that really matters. If we look forward to a dinner party and make all necessary arrangements to get there, in hopes of enjoying turtle soup, roast duck, and conversation with dear old George; our anticipation is no whit less worthwhile—no more "wrong"—if we have smoked salmon, partridge, and conversation with good old John. If we prepare for heaven in terms of imagery from the Apocalypse, we shall not be "wrong" if we discover at last that it is all rather different.

If atoms are postulated because there is something too small to see, then personal symbolism is applied to God because he is too big to know; it is the same principle. But I can only conclude with the original alternatives: I can assure the ordinary Christian that he need not worry over this point, and if that is unacceptable, he can make the necessary private study from the standard philosophical works.

12

CONTINGENCY IN MODERN LIFE

God is not bound to his own ordinances—but we are.
BISHOP GORE
But the Word of God is not bound.
2 TIM. 2.9

AT FIRST SIGHT it looks as though Rule, pattern and balance in prayer require, if not necessarily an ideal background, then at least a constant one; to St Benedict, *stability* was almost as important as poverty, chastity, and obedience as his basis for the *Regula*. And amid the complexities of modern life, and the diverse traditions of Anglicanism, this is rarely to be enjoyed. What happens for example, when a Regular Christian family moves from one parish to another—possibly of very different tradition? Or when a man's business takes him away from home for long periods of the year? Or even when we are frequently away from our parishes at weekends? Compared with the stability of other ages, I think we must accept this peculiarly modern contingency as unideal, it is a difficulty to be overcome if not a nuisance to be borne. And a closer look at the problem shows that Rule can still be a help rather than a complication.

We must remember throughout the wise words which head this chapter; where possible we are bound to the ordinances of God, and we are wise to heed the ascetical experience of the Church's tradition, yet Grace knows no bounds. The anticlerical who asks what happens to a Churchman cast ashore on a desert island is asking a silly question because it fails to consider the more simple significance of the word "God", and most Christians would be able to cope with such a situation very well. Yet the Proficient member of a flourishing parish often finds it much more difficult when he is cast ashore in a tiny village or an isolated parish of uncongenial tradition. This can make things more difficult but advance is never impossible, and adverse circumstances have their own special opportunities; "the Word of God is not bound". If it were argued that this virtually makes normal Rule unnecessary and all that is ever required is for us to do our best without it, then Bishop Gore has given the first answer at the head of this chapter. And the second is that this argument hints at a sterile "bare necessity to salvation" outlook in which I—and I hope the reader—have no interest. We want to advance in adventure, and use all means at our disposal: if all the normal means are not at our disposal, we still want to advance.

I

I do not wish to enter into controversy with other schools of thought within my own communion, yet neither must I evade pastoral facts. I do not think there need be any argument that the spirit of Rule, ascetic and direction, of the Church as three-fold organism, and of the balanced combination of Office, Holy Communion and private devotion, contains a good deal that is alien to Protestantism, yet nothing that is contrary in form or spirit to the Book of Common Prayer. But for this reason it is much more difficult for the evangelical Churchman who finds himself in a Catholic parish than for a Christian Regular who finds himself in an Evangelical one. And I must reluctantly admit that, apart from a plea for an honest examination as to what is conviction and what is prejudice, I have nothing very helpful to offer the former. When the latter position is seriously examined, the chances are that an objective emphasis on the public Office is the only fundamental part of Rule to be omitted altogether, and, although it is unideal, the Office can be, and invariably is, recited privately.

The Proficient in such case will be familiar enough with Low Mass—or a plain celebration of the Lord's Supper—and although he will miss more worthy liturgy, the theology of the Church should carry him over this omission. Private prayer obviously remains unimpaired, and the bones of Rule remain. I am not of course underestimating the value and goodness of proper liturgy, but I think we must sometimes try to realize that a diamond remains a diamond whether set in platinum or cast iron. Rule, leading to a proficient, businesslike approach to religion, itself guards against that superficial "Catholicism" which falls to pieces whenever things are "not quite what we are used to".

But, although it is quite possible to make a constructive Rule based on one Mass a week, I think more frequent celebrations must be politely requested when reasonably needed. Lack of perspective is very apparent when the heathen brazenly insists on being "married in Church", everyone instructs the Vicar how to do his job, or seeks him out for work that is nothing to do with it; while the Faithful remain reticent in asking for the sacraments which are their right. Without arrogance, one Proficient in one parish has every right to demand Mass on Red-Letter Days and the daily public Office. But this is very pessimistic, for by the grace of God the need for such requests is decreasing very rapidly, and there must be very few parishes in England where, irrespective of tradition or colour, the Proficient Churchman would not be welcomed with open arms and find himself with a hard but absorbing job. And he must realize that the less healthy his parish, the smaller the communicant roll, the lower the general spiritual level, then the greater the responsibility Our Lord is thrusting upon him. Healthy parochial joy can still be one of God's little sweetmeats bestowed upon his weaker children; more blessed are those who can do without them.

The urban problem is simpler in one way and more difficult in another. Simpler because parochial boundaries are less rigid and there may be some freedom of choice as to the parish community to which one is to belong. But I think there is a deep theological implication in geography—residence in a parish means much more than mere convenience or proximity to a church building—and I would argue that only in extremely difficult circumstances should "the church at which one habitually worships" be other than a man's parish church by residence (see my *Pastoral Theology: a Reorientation*, pp. 14ff., etc.). Again I feel that serious Rule, the getting down to the efficient backbone of Christian living, should wean us away from mere fussiness. It can only be a lack of real prayer whereby so many devout souls become worried by the most absurdly trivial whims and fancies about absurdly trivial things.

But in spite of this exhortation, and my optimism that in modern Anglicanism the very worst is not very likely, it might be wise to prepare for it as far as possible. What do we do if the normal ministrations of the Church are not available, or if they are partially or temporarily withheld? I think there are four possible courses which might at least alleviate the position.

(1) I must confess that I have never been very happy about "spiritual communion" as commonly taught. Personally I find it exceptionally difficult to practise and a little difficult to explain in theology; but it remains a tradition more important and considerably more venerable than I am. Others might find it a workable substitute when the Mass is not available.

(2) But "spiritual communion" normally involves a willed spiritual and imaginative association with a particular Mass at a particular altar and, presumably, with a known group of Christians. That seems simply a recognition of the unity of the Mass and the unity of the Body of Christ, or the unity of the Church both universal and local. Again speaking personally, the "act of spiritual communion" seems to be superfluous; plainly God can use exercises of this sort as means of grace, but they constitute a means other than "Holy Communion". Be that as it may, we are in any case very near to a straightforward vicarious representation when one soul is asked to represent another at the Altar; to go to Mass for, on behalf of, someone who is unable to be present in person. And this is certainly a legitimate second best to be used instead of, or in conjunction with, spiritual communion.

(3) Following from this, association with a religious community or society through common Rule, so far as possible, can be a great help. In difficult circumstances of isolation and loneliness, even a list of names can bring some local corporate sense into prayer. I am forced to insist strongly on the theological importance of parish geography, yet an *occasional* visit to the nearest local Catholic centre is surely legitimate when

circumstances are really bad, and if some kind of local "fellowship" springs out of it there seems no reason why this should not be used as in these three points. Circumstances could be so difficult as to demand the expedient of enrolment on the Electoral Roll of some other parish, but I think such a merely legal convenience should be treated as something of a last resort.

(4) Whatever the difficulties and methods chosen to combat them, it is both helpful and necessary to keep rigidly to the Kalendar. This more than anything keeps the soul firmly and consciously within the corporate Body. When the Mass or Office is not provided, or is inaccessible, whether we choose "spiritual communion" or vicarious representation, the actual liturgical day, be it feast or feria, is always to be respected. Our private prayer and recollection should ensure our missing not "Sunday" or "Thursday" but Epiphany II, or the Thursday after Lent III or St Lucy's Day. It is hard to exaggerate the value and help of this little technique.

II

Within Anglicanism there is, however, much more subtle divergence than liturgical use and theological colour, which unduly upsets souls not only when they change parishes but when incumbents change, or even in circumstances offering as much stability as we can reasonably hope for. However God-ward, humble and self-effacing an incumbent may be, the parish cannot but bear something of the stamp of his personality, and I cannot agree that this is a very bad thing.

There is for example, the meticulously efficient parish where liturgy is performed to perfection, the congregation is drilled with military precision, and never a chair, book or hassock is a half-inch out of place. It will be efficient and worthy, it could be legalistic, but more probably "tension" is the greater danger.

Then there is the "homely" or "Christian family" type of parish where things are much easier, even "slap-dash", mistakes are made which nobody seems to mind, and the church looks invitingly untidy; it is the Christian common room rather than the works' office. There is no laxity or dirtiness—for which there can be no excuse whatever—but a laudable approach to the faith as an ordinary part of ordinary life. Books and hassocks all over the place could mean laziness, yet they could also mean that the church has been freely used and will be used again very shortly.

There is the parish where silence is kept for a period before and after Mass and where talk is always whispered; it is devout and efficient, not "unfriendly". To go to a strange church where "everyone looked serious and nobody spoke to me" probably means the presence, rather than the lack, of real love and joy. And there are parishes where the Mass concludes with animated chatter and peals of laughter, again this could mean a lack of understanding and piety, or it could manifest a healthy lack of mock-devout tension; a sort of efficient freedom from religious inhibition.

There are parishes of "evangelistic" approach and those of an objective Godwardness. There are those consciously struggling and those quietly pleased with themselves: those where nothing has changed for forty years and those where nothing seems to be done in the same way twice.

Naturally I have my own preferences in all these various attitudes but my one point here is that my own preferences, like those of anyone else, are singularly unimportant; in fact all this subtle divergence is a help rather than a hindrance to Christian growth. Any sort of maturity demands a certain humility, resilience, and loyalty; however much things conflict with our own temperament, we are on a very lowly spiritual level if they are allowed to become obsessive. The tidy-minded Christian who is really upset by a jumble of books and hassocks, the "devout" who is angered by laughter in church, and their opposite numbers, are on the kindergarten level of those who cannot say their prayers amid the slightest distraction. But I think there is far more in it than this.

Personality evolves from relationships, and society, community, corporateness, are all things that grow out of the solution of frictions—of "value-resistances". The real community sense of an organization, firm or club, is not achieved by their members being identical in temperament or outlook, but by sinking necessary frictions into a primary common interest. There is always the awkward boss, manager or foreman, whose foibles rankle but common interest and maturity overcome them, which is itself a strengthening process. Marriage and family life deepen through such a communal give and take, and contrary to popular opinion, the best of religious communities are made up of much divergence of personality. Thus it seems tragic that men and women who accept all this as normal and necessary to creative living are put out by the slightest deviation and distraction in parochial affairs. And it seems not unfair to suspect the lack of the really deep common interest, that is of common Rule and the creative work of prayer; as being the fundamental cause. Proficiency demands the purposeful cultivation of at least some measure of resilience and humility in facing these annoying yet creative little irritations. We must, I think, try loyally to enter into the spirit and tradition of a parish community and not merely put up with the aspects of it that run counter to our own foibles. Scrupulosity can enter into liturgy and parochial outlook as well as ascetic and morals, and it remains a serious spiritual disease. In short, the man who rejects his own parish church for one that "suits him better" might be missing a great deal more than he gains.

III

We do not live in a Catholic society and one of the most difficult personal decisions is the choice between a firm insistence on duty and the requirements of charity, or even good manners. And I am doubtful if the unbendable choice of the first alternative is in all cases the right one, or that it furthers the Christian cause in terms of "witness" quite so much as some assume. Should nurses, 'bus drivers, dairymen, and domestics refuse orders which conflict with a Red-Letter Day Mass? or does the guest of a country house party insist on upsetting every arrangement of staff and household in order to hear Mass on Sunday morning, or is he bound to refuse all invitations that might conflict with religious duty? All such decisions must finally be made by the soul concerned, and they can be extremely delicate ones—or of course they can be made in direction, if need be by acts of holy "obedience". But there are I think, certain principles relating to theological proficiency which can give considerable guidance, and at least help to base such decisions on something a little firmer than convention or untrained "conscience". We are up against the contingencies of modern life, especially the rigid time-schedules by which the modern world functions, which make the example of other ages—especially the era of the New Testament—practically irrelevant. In these problems I think we must be bold enough to look at theology before tradition, and at both together before self-imposed ideals.

It is not always appreciated how much the love of God is manifested in the paradox that the Mass is far and away the greatest act that ever happens on earth, yet at the same time it is amongst the simplest and most easily available. When we really think of what the Mass is, and what it does, all other worldly works and problems seem insignificant, which suggests that this greatest of all values should take precedence over all other things whatsoever. Thus it is argued that if there were only one Mass a month—as in some parts of the mission field—then it would be more truly appreciated and we should make sure that nothing interfered with it. But I think this is false reasoning because if it were anywhere near the mind of Christ, he could have instituted a means of sacramental Grace which was much more difficult to perform and was much less easily available. All such speculation is really worthless, the fact remains that the greatest gifts and privileges (the Sacrament of Penance is another obvious example) are there for the asking, and this is God's arrangement not ours. Hence the seemingly paradoxical ruling of the Church that, in emergencies, works of charity take precedence over devotion, is pastoral and not Pelagian. To what extent the daily routine of nurses and 'bus drivers, or consideration for heathen hostesses or pagan hoteliers, are "works of charity" is a question upon which I would not care to generalize, and which must finally depend on particular circumstances. But it rather looks as if Our Lord, in his wisdom and humanity, is prepared to make considerable allowance for the mundane contingencies of the twentieth century.

There is another paradox: although the Kalendar is more than an expediency—for it eternally links the Church Militant with the Church Triumphant—nevertheless there is a sense in which High Mass on Ascension Day is exactly the same *thing* as the Low Mass of a feria. Although special obligation and significance attach to the great festivals, Sunday's parish communion is the same thing as the Low Mass of Monday. Roast turkey and plum pudding in January is not "Christmas dinner", but it is the same *thing*; equally stimulating and nourishing. And as Dr Mascall points out in his *Corpus Christi*, it is not so much "parish Communion", however impressive it may look, that gives the greatest theological expression to the fact of Christian corporate unity, but half a dozen groups hearing Mass at six altars in one church. Similarly there is unity and loyalty parochially expressed by the six weekday Masses each attended by a different communicant, and in small parishes there may be the rather odd paradox whereby an individual's lone attendance on Monday may add more to parochial efficiency than his dutiful and obviously right observance of the Sunday festival. Without claiming to give any clear cut answer to particular problems, I think all this constitutes a legitimate guiding factor when contingencies such as the weekend house party arise. What some would be tempted to call the lax view might also be the most efficient.

Occasions will doubtless arise when Christians are called upon to decide in favour of duty with courage and sacrifice, and it is heartening to see how frequently such decisions are made; but it is also tragic to notice how often heroic sacrifice is made for conventional and wholly insufficient reasons. Rule, and the conception of prayer in terms of theological efficiency, again help us see things in clearer perspective. For instance, great sacrifice has been made, to the extent of dismissal from lucrative work and consequent family hardship, in support of the Sabbatarian heresy—and let us for goodness' sake call this particular spade a spade. It seems quite tragic when those heroically defiant against "Sunday work" would never dare ask their employer for ten minutes' grace in order to hear the Maundy Thursday Mass, and might even miss the Sunday

Mass with far less heartsearching. Whatever the moral scruples involved—and here I am afraid that "scruples" is the right word—Sabbatarian practices can add nothing whatsoever to the efficient functioning of the Body of Christ. It would be very much more sensible, and far truer "witness", to refuse Saturday night's party in favour of proper observance of Sunday's vigil, or to make corresponding sacrifices on the authority of the Lenten fast.

Again, though with a little more justification, many a hard-working family has foregone a healthy day off in the sunshine for the sake of Sunday's Evensong at the parish church. This is much more subtle, and virtues like corporate responsibility and loyalty could be involved, yet with the strain and tension of modern life I think we must ask what is the efficient difference between "Sunday Evensong" and the Office said privately at home or on the beach—especially if this is the family's normal rule. What indeed is the essential difference, if any, between the evening Office of Sunday and that of any other festival? And is there any particular value in the corporate Office once a week anyway? The analogy between the spiritual efficiency of the local Body of Christ and the commercial efficiency of a factory can be overstrained, yet surely some attention should be paid to the best use of a busy layman's time. And I must submit, in all fraternal charity, that parish clergy are apt to be thoughtless in this respect.

According to tradition and theology, two Masses, seven Offices, and four hours' private prayer a week, plus actual recollection, is a very full Rule for the busy layman to undertake. Yet such a Rule could be kept by a man who, in difficult domestic or professional circumstances, might give a superficial impression of comparative laxity. He might hear low Mass on Sunday, another before travelling to work on Wednesday, and say his Office privately—and he would not be "seen at Church very often". Another man who went to church four times on Sundays, ran the Youth Club, kept the accounts and played the organ, and expected the church to be shut up for the rest of the week, would probably be looked on more favourably by many an incumbent. Yet it is hard to conceive greater ascetical inefficiency.

In view of all we hear about Anglican liberty and individualism, it is remarkable how loyal and obedient our laity are—which is another reason why I think so many are longing and groping for Proficiency. So should we not be a little more careful to put ascetical balance before superficial appearances in making demands upon them? Before talking glibly about the "duty" of Sunday Evensong, or of extra-Regular and extra-liturgical functions to which "all the faithful are expected", should we not stop to ask ourselves exactly what all this is going to add to the Redemption of the world through the action of the Body of Christ?

Let us by all means keep that proper perspective which puts the Adoration of God before all other values, and which gives our heavenly citizenship prior civic rights. May we live with heroism and sacrifice in the service of Christ, but with prudence, balance and humility. There is little virtue in "martyrdom" that is self-imposed by personal whim, and time can be wasted in church as well as anywhere else.

IV

Because Grace knows no bounds, the Christian life can be creatively lived in all possible circumstances—even the desert island—when the normal means are withdrawn. That is the real meaning of authoritative "dispensation", which is not the easy let-off from dull duty of popular misconception, but an occasion when theology and experience suggest that God is likely to provide extra-sacramental grace. And there are two such contingencies which the Church has always recognized; old age and the mission field, which, although obviously pertaining to all ages, have special relevance to our own.

I do not think modern Anglicanism is guilty of any serious neglect of her aged faithful, and it is obvious that any undue rigour here would be out of place and uncharitable. But in view of the "theological contingency" of age and infirmity, could it be that our ministrations to it are unduly negative? It is plain to any with but slight pastoral experience that God frequently grants very special powers and graces to the elderly, thus forming an efficient spiritual force which is not always given its true value.

In one of Miss Dorothy Sayers' novels, Lord Peter Wimsey discovers that, because of their frailty, lack of suspiciousness, and propensity for idle gossip, old ladies could be usefully employed in the field of crime detection. Analogously and rather more seriously, have we not here a very under-employed power—a sort of parochial spiritual labour force—which we estimate in worldly rather than spiritual-efficiency terms? There is always the vulgar jibe that clergymen spend most of their time looking after old ladies; yet when this is considered, here is a group of experience, maturity, a general lack of worldly ambition and temptation, stability, very special gifts of grace, and not infrequently a frustrating sense of boredom and uselessness. Efficiency in prayer is a concept with a disconcerting habit of overturning ordinary values and I rather feel that some are in for a shock when, in the Church Expectant, we discover the real perspective of power for world redemption; the achievements of the Prime Minister and Foreign Secretary may look pretty small compared with the influence wrought by little Mrs Perkins of Honeysuckle Cottage. My point is that parish efficiency still depends on Rule and direction, but here is a vitally important group of "contingent" circumstances wherein normal ascetical doctrine and techniques do not apply, or need very considerable adaptation.

Conversely, are we not just a little thoughtless in our enthusiasm for a congregation of "young people" or in our superficial assumption that Sunday schools are "the Church of the future"? If the Church is the Glorified Humanity of Christ, if spiritual progress and maturity are possible ideals, and if the efficient functioning of the Body of Christ in obedience means anything at all, then these glib sentiments are so much nonsense. Give me the old ladies any time.

The mission field is obviously a sphere which is both blessed by God and is intrinsically outside the working of normal Rule. And I think it can be defined as an area where the Church is in process of being, but is not as yet, fully established. The point here is that there are many such areas in our own country and it would both aid efficiency and assist the faithful if we were bold enough to admit this fact and act accordingly.

I would tentatively suggest that where there is no Red-Letter Day Mass and regular daily Office, there is no "parish" in the sense of the local microcosm of the Body of Christ, and there are whole Rural Deaneries in isolated districts where this is the case. If facts were faced and such areas frankly called "mission districts" the faithful—whom I tried to help in section I of this chapter—would be helped very much more. All the traditional ascetical modifications and "dispensations" would be brought into play, and these faithful, not forgetting the parish priest—or rather "mission" priest—would at least know where they stood. I submit that this is far more than an argument about names and words, for even on a modest pastoral level, a progressive mission district is surely better than a series of dead "parishes", and there would be both a clear personal duty and a worthy corporate ideal—true "parish status"—at which to aim.

13

CHRISTIAN MATURITY IN THE WORLD

> You are a sort of imposter when your profession and practice disagree.
>
> ST AMBROSE

> The heavens are not too high,
> His praise may thither fly;
> The earth is not too low,
> His praises there may grow.
> Let all the world in every corner sing,
> My God and King!
>
> GEORGE HERBERT

IDEALS ARE easier to describe than to achieve, though they are not always too easy to describe, and Christian ideals are apt to degenerate into shadowy sentiment. Many discussions about Christian behaviour rotate around something like my quotation from St Ambrose, and it would be argued that if a man goes to Church he must not fiddle his income-tax returns, or if he says his prayers he must not say a good many other words. Without belittling the importance of financial honesty and decent language, I think we must assume that there is rather more in it than that, and I would say that the words quoted from George Herbert give a much deeper expression of what "practical Christianity" really means. The Christian Proficient is both a citizen of the heavenly country and very much a man of this world, and it is the resolution of this paradox, which gives rise to several others, that produces sane Christian maturity. As we saw in the last chapter, Christians are called upon to make prudent decisions, sometimes of sacrifice and renunciation, in defence of their profession, but these decisions are not always as clear-cut as convention would suppose. What a Christian should, or should not do, does not always agree with popular ethics, or even popular Christian ethics; the laws of the New

Jerusalem are not always consistent with the laws of Liverpool. As ever, we must have recourse to the pastoral application of theology.

I

What we do depends upon what we are, Christian behaviour depends upon what a Christian is, Christian action is the action of Christ himself expressed in and through the malleable members of his Mystical Body. Thus the Adoration of God in the Sacraments is the most morally perfect "Christian" activity there can be, for a Christian is, essentially and by definition, a soul incorporated into the glorified humanity of Christ by Baptism. So as we have seen, the real "hypocrite" is the baptized soul who rarely makes his communion—however impeccable his "moral" character may be—for he is living a continuous lie against the ultimate, eternal truth of his profession. This truth must never be forgotten, and yet, by now familiar theology, this supernatural status is to find expression on a worldly level. Because we are incorporated, not "absorbed", into Christ, because we are made responsible sons and not servile tools, we are to seek personal manifestation of our status by prudent decision, free will, and moral struggle. Because we are *in* Christ and he is *in* us, we *are* Christians—come what may and behave as we will—yet we want to be good Christians, we are to try to be "Christ-like" in life.

Now "Christ-like" is a term more subject than most to sentimental and over-"devotional" vagary. And there seem to be three stages in which, or through which, we must examine this term before it makes very much pastoral sense. First, it is right to feel that the Person of Jesus whom we meet in meditation, and converse with in colloquy, is the most perfectly attractive of all personality; whom we desire to imitate without a lot of theological analysis. But we soon confront our original paradox in the form of a divine Being who, though despising the "world", is lovingly at home with the creation. And when we really face up to Christ as Person rather than "meditating" around one or two devotional ideas, we find all the other paradoxes common to human personality; in Christ there is love and also anger, compassion and also rigour, simplicity and profundity, humour and tears, joy and sorrow, obedience and rebellion, stern duty and light-hearted gaiety. Yet lists of characteristics do not make a Character.

Secondly, we must realize that no man's meditation is fully adequate to comprehend Christ perfectly, or even accurately. Essential as our own meditation is—despite its inadequacy—we need the guidance of the total meditative experience of the Church to tell us clearly what the "Christ-like" qualities really are; and this is the living basis of moral theology. Thus the categories of the text-books, the cardinal and theological virtues, the evangelical counsels, and the gifts of the Spirit: are no academic jingles but the results of the Church's thought on her corporate mental prayer. If we need lists of qualities to help us and to aim at, the truest we can say is that Jesus Christ is Just, Temperate, Prudent, and possessed of Fortitude (the cardinal virtues); that his earthly life was governed by Faith, Hope, and Love (the theological virtues); that he adored the Father in Holy Fear, Reverence, and Godliness, he offered the world Wisdom, Understanding, Knowledge, and Counsel, and that these were derived from Ghostly Strength (the gifts of the spirit). And the more we ponder this list the more obvious it becomes that the world's view of what is really "Christ-like" does not coincide with the experience of the Church. The more our personal meditation is guided by this knowledge, the more reliable its fruits will be and the more Christ-like our personal decision and worldly judgement.

But, thirdly, we have still little more than a list of characteristics, even if a more accurate one. If we have moved from a general vagueness to a general conciseness, we must move one stage further to a particular conciseness. We must try, by guided meditation and colloquy, to discover how Our Lord would have the Christ-like virtues manifested in our own unique personality.

We come to a theological paradox of considerable pastoral importance and practical value, neglect of which is responsible for much of the vagueness, sentiment, and muddle that we are trying to overcome. On the one hand Jesus Christ recapitulates, sums up, or embraces within himself, the whole human race; he is literally the Second Adam, father of the new creation: in fact he is Humanity. But he is also *a* Person with *a* perfectly human nature, and one essential characteristic of human personality is unique individuality; so the human nature of Christ is uniquely his own. Any other view would be playing into the hands of our old enemy, Apollinarianism. So although we can, by grace, strive to become "Christ-like", there is a sense in which we cannot be, and it is not impious to say we should not try to be, "like Christ". To be truly "Christ-like", in other words, means to try to become what Christ wants us, individually and uniquely, to be. On the purely human level—and this analogy has dangers if pressed too far—it is good for us to be influenced by the example of those better and greater than ourselves, but it is not conducive to integrity slavishly to copy the characteristics of others. There is something weak and unworthy about the "hero-worshipper" who, neglectful of his own qualities, apes those of another. The practical point is that to be "Christian" is not simply to "copy" Christ but to be incorporated into him by the initiatory Sacraments, which add to, but in no way diminish, personality. Human nature is to be super-naturalized but not standardized, and to think otherwise is no great compliment to a Creator who, it is insinuated, might have made a better job of standardization in the first place. If it were not for these facts, the New Testament would become the sole *literal* guide to Christian life in the modern world—which is a mistake many make in varying degrees of subtlety. The logical conclusions would be that marriage, riding a horse, or writing books, not to mention driving a car or working in a factory, are "unChrist-like" because they are not literally "like Christ", for he never did any of them. Nor are we far from the Apollinarian heresy if we argue that it is all right to be angry occasionally provided that we are loving and compassionate rather more frequently, because that seems to be how Christ behaved. We are still failing to think in terms of real Personality which though a complex of characteristics, is something much more than the sum of them.

This boils down to the very common fallacy that the "Christian" or the Christian "character" is some clearly defined "type", or that Christian behaviour is a standard pattern with which all Christians are stamped. Much as we reject this view in theory, much as we applaud St Peter of Cluny's "diversity in unity is the principle of Christendom", most of us are delightedly surprised when a professional boxer or a beautiful actress turns out to be a Proficient Christian; they are not quite "true to type". Truly all professions and circumstances have their particular temptations, but they also have their particular proportions of Christian qualities; if there is nothing unChrist-like in driving a car or marriage, then nor is there in being an efficient man of business, or a film star, or in knowing how to order a good dinner.

Similarly, Christian "witness" and "example" are too often interpreted in terms of "typical" behaviour of a rather superficial kind; of refusing to buy a raffle ticket or being something of a wet blanket at a party. Yet the invariable answer to "should a Christian do this, that or the other?" is, strangely, "it all depends". Christian life in the world flows not so much from outside "principles" as from habitual recollection; we are still concerned more with facts than with appearances. And I would suggest that the mature Proficient is one who follows his natural bent just in so far as it is consistent with habitual recollection; the man of affairs, the professional sportsman, the belle of the ball, who in their full and varied activities never lose sight of the Presence of God.

Maturity in any context is exemplified by humility, reserve, self-effacement; if there is no such thing as a "typical" Christian, then neither can there be an "obvious" one. The Proficient lives sacramentally, he is truly at home both in the world and in the oratory, his spiritual life is an ordinary thing, and the more "ordinary" it is the better. It is all a question of acknowledging a status rather than of striking a pose.

II

Sacramentalism, as general philosophy, is the principle of the Incarnation. Expressed pastorally and practically, it is the resolution of the paradox of the supreme self-sacrifice of a gluttonous man and a wine-bibber; of a Righteous Man who loved sinners; of the murdered redeemer of murderers. And it follows that both the zeal of the total abstainer and the shallowness of the "muscular Christian", the grimness of the Puritan and the false gaiety of the antinomian; are above all —whatever they may be besides—immature in spirit.

The relation between Christian dogma and practice is, rather strangely, that between the rigid and the elastic; thus the Mass can be celebrated in different ways, at different places, and in different ages, while remaining essentially the same thing. The Creeds contain eternal and objective truth, yet faith in them is expressed uniquely in every Christian life. And although moral theology is grounded in this dogma, the Church consistently refuses to adopt any legalistic code. It is dogmatically insistent that stealing is sinful, yet it does not maintain that a theft of money by a rich man and the theft of a loaf by the starving mother of children is the *same* thing; it will have nothing to do with a "categorical imperative" of an ethicist like Kant. Sane casuistry insists that circumstances alter cases, and it faces up to the facts of a world frequently demanding a choice of evils. Thus the really mature Christian becomes one who is dogmatically certain about dogma and lovingly liberal about practically everything else. He is unshakably firm about his supernatural status, about eternal truth, and about the creative primacy of spiritual things; he remains charitably sceptical about the ways of the world. In other words, Christian maturity expresses itself in a supernaturalized brand of balance, levelheadedness, proportion and perspective. It is sacramental.

The Puritan or Manichee looks on prime beefsteak as a snare of the devil; the worldling as almost the reason for life; to the Christian it is a creature of God forming part of the divine economy of his own life, to be treated with a certain respect and enjoyed with thanksgiving.

The traditional Quaker maid covers herself with the most voluminous and ugliest possible vesture of unrelieved black, while her shallow sister of the world thinks of nothing but "fashion". To the Christian lady, clothes can be as sacramental as anything else, they constitute something which can pleasingly express spirituality, that can be a quite joyful sign of the glory of God's intricate creation. "Let *all* the world in *every* corner sing: My God and King."

There are still duties of stewardship, of almsgiving, and of modesty; there are still sins of luxury, gluttony, and concupiscence: but Christian life remains one of balance not fanaticism, of paradox not contradiction. And its personal details can only be worked out by the circumstances of recollected life, guided by the Holy Spirit in Prayer; there must be Rule and there cannot be "rules". And that is why studies in "Christian sociology" or "Christian ethics" or "Christian" anything else, divorced from Prayer and the ontological significance of Baptism, must suffer from the ineffectiveness of the immature. Being is prior to becoming; what a thing *is* decides what it does: therefore Christian morals cannot exist without the basis of Christian ascetic.

III

Maturity of Spirit, as of other things, involves level-headedness, proportion and balance, but of a far greater richness and depth than the philosophy of "moderation in all things". The comparatively inexperienced Christian may manifest an effervescent enthusiasm for not getting drunk, possibly to the extent of temperance campaigns, which prove both ineffective and tedious. The more mature will have developed a greater love for, and a loathing for the misuse of, the creatures of God—including himself; and the more fully mature, striving towards habitual recollection, learns spontaneously to accept or reject in accordance with the needs of his prayer. The unharnessed zeal of youth, hasty and imprudent, leads to excesses one way or the other: antinomianism or legalism, gluttony in all its forms or Puritanism. And we have seen that even in prayer leading to Adoration—which can hardly be excessive—deeper and more lasting fulfilment grows from balance and proportion.

By spiritual truth absorbed into itself, Christian maturity is the living resolution of a set of paradoxes. Anxiety, despair, scrupulosity, and fussiness, have no place where God the Father reigns; yet life's smallest detail or tiniest creature is significant through the indwelling of the Holy Ghost. Because

Christ is God and Christ is man, penitence and joy, fear and love, faith and doubt, devotion and works, universal and particular, humanity and men; all combine into Adoration which eliminates none yet is greater than all. The world of commerce, art, education, politics, family, sorrow, pleasure, science and sociology; all is insignificant compared with the infinitely rich reality of God, yet all things are significant, including lobster salad and motor cars, because of the Incarnation, and for no other reason whatsoever.

The fact that there is no "typical" Christian personality, occupation or society—or even era—means that it is impossible to enter into any detailed discussion as to how dogmatic and moral theology are to be carried over into behaviour. But the basic question involved, the relation between the Christian and his community, is again to be answered by meditative consideration of Christ as Person; not merely his dealings with particular people in an historic situation, but his constant contemplative love and concord with creation coupled with his hatred of sin. In other words a consideration of Christ as Person within the general context of the doctrine of the Atonement. All the extremes we have just cited mean, in practice, a discordant relation with the world, a lack of "contemplative harmony" with and in creation. But how can we be in harmony with so much ugliness and sin? Only in Our Lord's own way; by constant concern for, and personal identification with, the world in travail—which is the general intercessory approach discussed on pp. 98–100.

The Pharisee of the parable saw sin and thanked God for his own righteousness. That was not hypocrisy but selfishness; he *was* righteous but he lacked love. The publican was concerned, I think, not only with his own sins but with all sin; he was a natural and constant intercessor, at one with all around him, anxious to share rather than condemn, to suffer rather than run away, to live sacrificially rather than exclusively. So Proficiency is incompatible with sectarianism, it may have to be bold enough to denounce sin, but much more is it willing to share its consequences sacrificially. That is the whole doctrine of Christ's Atonement carried over into his Mystical Body. And that is why the Proficient, in humility, suffering, intercession and compassion, must face up to the fact that he is "important"; not because of his own righteousness or qualities but because of his vocation to help work out Christ's redemptive plan.

IV

There are two further aspects of Christian life to which some attention must be given: evangelism and apologetic; and I think that here again the fallacy of over standardization of approach is much in evidence today.

Plainly what applies to the over literal interpretation of Our Lord's example of earthly life applies equally to his example as manifested in his infant Church. As Richard Meux Benson writes: "St Paul tells us that we must keep up many associations in the world, otherwise we must needs go out of it. We have to accept our position. God's call to successive ages is not the same. The principle remains unchanged, but the mode of exercising it varies indefinitely." In other words to "follow Christ" means that we must try to avoid the capital sins and cultivate the virtues in our own state, but it does not mean that none must marry and all should be carpenters. Similarly, to be consistent with the early Church means that we must honour the Creeds and live by the sacraments, but not that we should slavishly copy the details of life in First Century Palestine. All that sounds childishly obvious, yet I think it is true that as we think of evangelism today, despite all the books, tracts, and conferences on "modern methods", we still have St Paul's missionary journeys in the back of our minds. We still tend to imagine the Apostle in Athens, however much we are aware of the lack of a population with ingrained philosophic interests and nothing much to do.[1] And despite ignorance and misconception, the Faith today is scarcely "some new thing" and, even if it was, it would be treated by modern minds with a not unhealthy scepticism. The whole situation is so completely different that we must surely re-think the whole implication of proclaiming the Gospel to every creature; not only society but theology has developed and

[1] Acts 17. 21.

deepened. The need is for a consistently new, more mature approach rather than merely "new methods", and to substitute the television studio for Mars Hill does not seem to me to alter the basic method at all.

When the Christian has not only discovered the truth that gives life purpose, but absorbed it into personality by Rule over some years; evangelism becomes a developed instinct rather than an occasional duty. It is natural to wish to share our joy with others, to introduce them to the love of God; and we are all most rightly elated when we can prove of use in this way. But I would say that it is quite useless to think about lay-evangelists until this necessary grounding in Rule has led to a reasonable maturity of faith. Even then I cannot but feel that a great deal of evangelistic power is wasted by an underlying assumption of the "Mars Hill" method and no other. It must be admitted that there are open-air preachers and evangelistic visitors of particular gifts and zealous courage, and none would deny their right to develop and use such gifts for the glory of God. Yet I am equally bound to admit considerable doubt as to whether this is a fruitful technique for the modern situation; it is again the good enough fast bowler on the slow wet wicket. Society has reached that stage of sophistication which early Athens lacked; today we not unwisely distrust the bubbling enthusiasm and tenseness of a new convert, be it to religion, politics, music, or anything else. Such direct appeal implies either the short-lived enthusiasm of youth or the self-centredness of the bore; it is immature.

If the Church is a living organism, we can look upon its New Testament manifestation as its "infancy" by strict human analogy, it was possessed of childlike simplicity and purity but it still had to grow up and develop, even if, like men, it developed a good many regrettable tares along with the grain. And it is no detraction from the pure faith of the Apostolic Church to call it immature in this sense; it would be heretical if the liturgy, for example, lost all its roots in New Testament practice, yet it is both false and ingenuous to try to go back—and that is the right phrase—to that kind of simplicity. And the same applies to evangelism, so what is the true position now?

I think there are two inter-related preliminaries. First, that the main, if not the sole, evangelistic power is the efficient spirituality of the Catholic Church, which in fact replaced the earlier "missionary journey" technique. And secondly, which is much the same point in personal terms, that our own growth in prayer and spiritual perception exudes a joyous stability more attractive and influential than argument or exhortation. And further, our theology has advanced—and I think it is an advance—in looking on the Church as Christ's vicarious agency for world redemption rather than as the "ark of salvation" of more primitive times. We have returned to the truer tradition that puts Adoration, not soteriology, as the ultimate value. Because by this we conceive God as greater than his Church on earth, we can put all emphasis on the reality of sacramental grace without preaching, with St Augustine, the necessary damnation of all the unbaptized. Without in any way denying true zeal for the conversion of all men, we can nevertheless dispense with the over-zealous urgency of a more impetuously youthful outlook: we can wait on the Spirit and bide our time without laxity. "Prepare to meet thy doom, the end of the world is at hand" may be good advice based on a true statement, but its particular type of urgency is immature and ineffective because it fails to face the fact of God's omnipotence and transcendence. And the type of urgency expressed by reference to the chaotic state of the world and its dangers to the "church" makes no sort of sense if the Church is that glorified Humanity of Christ which cannot very well be in danger. We are still faced with the paradox of the Heavenly and earthly cities, but I do not think this view, held by Christian Regulars, can be called apathetic. It is rather the result of mature judgement and composure. In any case we are not going to "evangelize" the world in five minutes by any method, and there is little Christian witness in panic.

Are we to hold then that the Christian Proficient is to live to Rule, fall back on the redemptive activity of God through his Church, and leave it at that? If we did just that I think we should be doing far more truly evangelistic work than some would think, but we can go a step or two further.

Habitual recollection is never fully acquired in this life, and further effort is always to be made literally to carry Christ's presence into all worldly situations. Further, spirituality becomes not only contagious but sensitive as it deepens, and if a "Mars Hill" sermon is unlikely to have much lasting effect on a 'bus or in a pub; we can keep our spiritual eyes and ears attuned to our friends, neighbours, and acquaintances. The contemporary lay-evangelist (or priest evangelist for that matter) is, I suggest, less of a preaching missionary and more of a spiritual detective; a religious talent-scout nosing about the world for new blood. In our daily lives it soon becomes fairly obvious where the Holy Spirit is purposefully at work; as the director of souls has a fairly good idea who his spiritual children are likely to be long before any relation is established, so the Regular layman may sense those souls who are groping, perhaps subconsciously, for his spiritual help. I just cannot accept the possibility that any Proficient Christian, living modestly to the Rule of the Church, learning by grace to love without seeking reward, yet keeping his eyes on God's good creation, will fail to find a good deal of evangelistic work thrust upon him. Yet even here I would be bold enough to repeat that reticence, patience and composure—maturity in fact—is needed before urgent arrogance. In the ordinary process of spiritual awakening, of "conversion", souls are far more likely to be lost through impetuosity than by patience. But even when such a relation with another has been effected, when we have what is commonly called an "opening", are we really clear what personal "evangelism" means? The literal, public proclamation of the Gospel—the Mars Hill idea—barely recommends itself as suitable technique for personal influence. In fact my main criticism of the current preoccupation with "evangelism", and especially lay-evangelism, is the ambiguous panic that always seems to go with it; we are so constantly exhorted to "evangelize" with no clear idea of its meaning or method.

What I think ought to be meant, and what is occasionally hinted at, is something akin to that personal introduction to Christ of which St Paul speaks, not on Mars Hill but in the first Corinthian letter: "I am determined brethren to know (or make known) among you the Crucified Christ." "To know among you" is a very close personal relation that can mean nothing less than the introduction of one person to another, both of whom are on intimate terms with the mediator. "Charles, my dear fellow, may I introduce my old friend Henry" implies my own deep understanding and friendship with both. Now compare the more mundane experience; when a boy in my parish whom I have nodded to once or twice asks me for a "reference" to an employer I have never met. I might write down that so far as I know the boy is clean, honest, and well behaved, or more honestly that I have no evidence to the contrary; all of which means little or nothing. The point is that this is not a personal introduction, yet I fear that it is the kind of thing so often suggested by "evangelism"; we are back to the lecture on a list of characteristics—Jesus is good, merciful, forgiving, our Saviour, Son of God—all of which is true enough but it is a "reference", not an introduction of person to Person. So again, by logic rather than piety, meditation within Rule is the first, most practical and essential need if evangelism is to mean anything real; we must really *know* Christ as Person before we can introduce him to others. The only consistent way to "train lay-evangelists" is to guide their mental prayer within in the framework of the Church's Rule.

As we noticed in Chapter 10, Proficients really ought to talk about prayer as naturally and easily as they speak of baking a cake or catching a train; it is a much commoner and more ordinary thing than either. Similarly, holy souls sometimes speak of Jesus just as they speak of their brother or best friend; sometimes it sounds irreverent and shocking but then holiness usually shocks people. But in conversation with such souls there is never the slightest doubt about the real presence of Christ as living Person; it is different from an argument about theology or a discussion about a list of qualities: it is neither a sermon nor a "reference" but a personal introduction. Christ does condescend to use us—that is what Baptism means—and in spite of our inadequacy, stupidity, frailty, and sin, he uses us to introduce himself to others. He can shine through our dull and uninspiring personalities, but only when we are in him, and when we try to allow him into us. That, I suggest, is what "lay-evangelism" really means, and it is why humility and reticence succeed better than arrogance and ingenuous "zeal".

V

A working knowledge of theology that can hold its own in debate and discussion is a great and good advantage, yet I am committed to the position that relieves the ordinary Proficient Christian of any such arduous study unless it particularly interests him. And the solution of this deadlock is, I think, that we are inclined to interpret "Christian apologetic" on the comparatively shallow level of argument. This is to deny neither theology nor reason, and the intellectual apologetics of the early centuries of our era were a necessary stage in the Church's development. So indeed is the continued study of modern theologians, and the more reason we can bring into our faith the better, both for ourselves and the world at large. But in the ordinary pastoral sense, apologetic means much more than "standing up for the faith" or trying to convince others of its truth or reasonableness; it means the living manifestation of that truth. We have already mentioned in one or two places in this book that life within the Church, life lived Regularly under the influence of grace and balanced prayer; demonstrates the meaning of the Church itself, and of the significance of Baptism as fact: over the more common misconceptions as to what Christianity really means. I have even suggested answers to the more usual criticisms and attacks, yet I do not believe for a moment that these right answers are going to be any more acceptable to the prejudiced and misinformed than the wrong views they already hold. Those who really think the Church is a social organization, or that it is concerned with Puritan ethics, or that it is either a kind of club you "go to" according to need or whim, or an autocratic power to which one submits; are not likely to give up their fond ideas however many arguments they "lose".

We must rather insist that religion, though reasonable, is not entirely or even mainly, a matter of intellect; yet to insist on "faith" rather than logic is less acceptable than anything to those who do not understand or know it. And I think the convinced Christian himself feels that the appeal to faith sounds rather weak and evasive. But the liberating influence of Rule may *demonstrate* truth far more capably than argument, and it at least shows—even proves—that Christianity is a living thing, a specific activity in its own right that one *does* and not just an external code that one holds. The comparatively immature talk about prayer with a rather wild enthusiasm, the Proficient cannot but impress others with its necessity and ordinariness. When, without stunt or artificiality, we can say "excuse me I must go and say some prayers" in the same manner as "excuse me I have a cake in the oven" I think we have reached the peak of really effective apologetic. And all this is made up by the mature characteristics: normality, ease, reticence; lack of tension, flurry and grimness.

Whatever our theology we cannot escape the particular, if passing, scandals of modern Christianity; its apparent ineffectiveness in social and international affairs, its necessary but regrettable superstructure of administration and finance, and worst of all, schism. But I still believe that to the proverbial man in the street, it does not *do* anything specific; it remains a conglomeration of theories, ethics, and conflicting codes of conduct. To think ascetically immediately produces a far bolder front. Without in any way condoning schism, there is a sense in which it can be regarded as that rich diversity of ascetical method hardly unknown in the undivided Church! "Which is right?" in terms of theory or "salvation" becomes "which is the most exciting and workable ascetical scheme?" We can be Anglicans because we believe we are the Catholic Church of this land, indeed we must insist on this; but in terms of pastoral apologetic we can be Anglicans because we have a localized, and in the right sense "nationalized", system of ascetic which suits us and which "works".[1] There seems no reason to deny a slightly different system to those of other

[1] However rich the spiritual diversity of Christendom, however valuable, popular, and exciting is the teaching of St Bernard, St Ignatius, St Teresa, or St François: it is important for Anglicans to remember that there is a specifically *English* school of universal importance.

lands, and I think we can more charitably approach Protestantism with a balanced type of ascetic, a scheme or system of *religion*, rather than endless arguments about doctrine. Instead of "Your doctrine of the Church is wrong" I would prefer "Without the Catholic doctrine of the Church, how do you intercede?" Rather than "We believe in 'set prayers' and you do not" I prefer "Without the Office how do you offer praise to God the Father?" Not "Confession is right and you are wrong" but "How do you combat aridity caused by sin?" It might almost be said that if imaginative or pictorial meditation is the key to modern Evangelism, then intellectual meditation—the *absorbing* of living truth—is the key to modern apologetic.

14

THE PROGRESS TO MATURITY: CONCLUSION

In the last chapter I tried merely to describe the characteristics of Christian maturity as it manifests itself to the world. And these were found to be, in the main, a unique personal "Christlikeness", a wide sacramentalism which resolves a series of paradoxes, and a sane unobtrusive zeal for evangelism and apologetic. But the whole point of an ascetical approach to religion is that it is practical and progressive. It cannot rest content with a bare recognition of ideals but must strive to follow the stages and processes through which they are attained. It is only by working out the experiences of childhood and adolescence that we become finally adult, and there is a similar spiritual growth, but in religion these three stages form a kind of "Hegelian triad" which for our purpose means the resolution of a paradox; that is, the combination of two seemingly contradictory things into a third thing which is greater than either. It is worth while looking at this general progress in three different but inter-connected ways.

(1) In his essay *Holy Worldliness*,[1] Dr A. R. Vidler sees it in terms of world-affirmation, world-renunciation, and a synthesis of these, as typified by David, John Baptist, and Our Lord Jesus Christ.

"We must all have noticed how hard and how ingeniously Christian divines have to work in order to find in the Old Testament even premonitions of a life, worthy of the name, beyond the grave, and we know that the doctrine of resurrection was a late importation into Judaism."[2]

We know that in the time of St Paul the Sadducees still denied resurrection,[3] which accounts for much of the

[1] *Essays in Liberality*, V. [2] Ibid., p. 101. [3] Acts, 17.31–2; 23.8; 26.7–8.

gruesomeness of Old Testament religion. If God's honour is to be upheld and his justice vindicated, and if this is possible only in the present world, then to call down the fire from heaven to consume his enemies and to slaughter those who sin against him is the only logical thing to do. Thus:

"I would suggest that the thesis of the Bible with regard to the life of this world—its primary and unsophisticated affirmation of the world—is exemplified in David whom we may take here as a paradigmatic figure. David in whom the physical and psychic vitalities are conspicuously present: David who was at once shepherd and psalmist and king: David who fought when it was necessary, with all his might, against powerful animals and powerful men; David who danced, with all his might, before the Ark of God: David the epic friend and the epic lover and the epic father (O Absalom, my son, my son): David the poet laureate and the beloved commander who would not drink of the water from the well of Bethlehem, for which he had longed, but poured it out unto the Lord: David who never lost his tenderness and *joie de vivre* though he had to cope with toughs like Joab: David whose soul 'was bound in the bundle of life' with the Lord his God and who was 'the man after God's own heart'."

But:

"If David is the paradigmatic representative of the primary Yes that the Bible says to the world, John the Baptist is the paradigmatic representative of the No that must always be said in the next breath."[1]

There is neither need nor time here to go further into the paradoxical attitude of Our Lord to the world around him. In this he was different from David and different from the Baptist while retaining similarities with both. But this is a problem to be worked out by meditative prayer enlightened by study, for which Dr Vidler's essay offers a good start. Suffice it to say that Jesus is neither sociologist nor hermit, *bon viveur* nor Puritan, antinomian nor legalist; and any personal religion that overstresses these attitudes is immature. But, as Dr Vidler points out, immaturity is not "wrong", thus the religious instruction of children—and I

[1] Ibid., pp. 101–3.

think most new converts—should be wholeheartedly world-affirming.[1] These young souls should be taught to revel in the world, to be interested in, to look at and love, *things*; long before they are subjected to a frightening list of "don'ts". Love for God's good creation precedes "thou shalt not" as David precedes the Baptist, and if the whole conception of progress is kept to the fore I think the ultimate Christian synthesis will evolve naturally. As I have tried to maintain elsewhere, following Dr F. R. Tennant, the "first form of contemplation"—the sense of "at-homeness" with the world—is a necessary prologue to the Christian revelation.

(2) Or the progression may be stated in terms of the aesthetic, the intellectual, and the sacramental, which bears the closest relation to the more familiar triad: emotion, intellect and will. The religious life frequently begins with that world-affirming experience sometimes called "the first form of contemplation" or the search for God in his creatures; natural religion is a logical prologue to the Christian revelation. Thus the initial characteristic of the newly converted may be widely aesthetic, he is inspired by the beauty in nature, by the glories of Gothic churches, and by Christian music and art. This is a good beginning if an unsatisfactory end; in time creatures become something of a nuisance, beauty becomes empty, it ceases to inspire and becomes a distraction; emotion and feeling are giving way to reason, unbridled enjoyment of this world is to be trained by intellect and moral discipline. And, if all goes well, a fully sacramental life emerges; all these things remain but they are caught up into a richer and more stable perspective. At this mature stage, we still use music in worship but we can manage without it, we still seek God in the woodlands but only through meeting him in prayer, we still love the Gothic cathedral but we are not unduly worried if it falls. We cease to seek God in his creatures but see all creation in God.

(3) To put things in more directly pastoral terms I think the triad might be stated: evangelism, ecclesiasticism, ascetic. We have already noticed how the first flush of enthusiasm for anything issues in an ingenuous desire to share it with others,

[1] Ibid., pp. 107–8.

and however good our motives we risk becoming bores; thus the professional sportsman is generally reticent and the "rabbit" annoyingly effusive, it is the child's instinctive reaction to a new discovery, interest or toy—"come and see what *I* have got".

When this particular enthusiasm wears thin it may well give way to a rather shallow interest in technicalities, and especially in liturgy; it is the stage of the "spike". Needless to say I am not suggesting for a moment that interest in either evangelism or liturgy or church administration is "wrong" any more than David or St John Baptist were "wrong", but that their respective over-emphases only combine into balanced maturity at a third fully Christian stage. And this, pastorally speaking, is what I call the ascetical approach, in which liturgy becomes the framework of a recollected life in the world and from which evangelistic influence flows. Again all things and all people are sought and seen in God, and service to others becomes the expression of life in Christ; service purified from self-interest or ecclesiastical "success".[1]

The difficulty of writing a book about ascetical theology, especially with regard to Rule and direction, is to try to avoid the impression that prayer is something impossibly complicated and rigid. We risk the danger of the farmer who, having read a treatise on the diseases of poultry, found it quite impossible to imagine a healthy hen. On the other hand, having tried to bring some sort of order into private prayer,

[1] In view of certain criticism (and I think misconception) of the "Remnant" concept of pastoral organization, perhaps a charitable point could be stretched to include this, with the alternative schemes I reject, in a similar triad. What I call "multitudinism"—the recruitment of as many as possible into the Church's life irrespective of any other consideration, with and through a host of social organizations and "attractions"—is certainly a "worldly" approach! Yet it might perhaps be a legitimate first stage in certain circumstances. I have also rejected the "exclusive" policy—the pious little clique or sect cut off from the world—yet again this could be but the other-worldly stage of the Baptist, or the hermit, or the "spike". But I still champion the Remnant as the higher synthesis of both. Discipline and Rule in, and vicariously on behalf of, the world; the unobtrusive recollection of God overflowing on to the world in service, suffering, love and joy, is the religion not of David, or of the Baptist, but of Christ. *See Pastoral Theology: a Reorientation.*

there may seem to be so many exceptions to the rule that the systems themselves fall to pieces. Similarly direction may sound horribly tight, restrictive and autocratic, or it may seem to be little more than having the parson for a friend. Yet this is only the principle of the Faith we have discussed in the last chapter; infinite pastoral elasticity springing from a firmly dogmatic foundation. And I can only assure the reader that, except in very unusual cases, Rule and direction can be applied to him and made exactly to fit his own unique temperament, outlook, and personality. And he will find them liberating and expansive, and much less complicated in practice than it might appear in theory. In spite of the weighty tomes on the diseases of poultry—which of course are very valuable and important—there are considerable numbers of healthy chickens. In fact there are more than there would be without all the books.

But I have done my poor best to avoid these extremes, and experience remains the only real test of its usefulness. If one reader is encouraged to experiment with Rule and direction, and to re-think his religious life in terms of workmanlike proficiency, then I do not think I shall have wasted my time.

Although for a book of this kind very little has been said about him, the Holy Ghost remains the ultimate director and guide, and the essential unifying principle behind our own modest efforts. But this has been a purposeful and I hope not irreverent omission. As St John of the Cross insists "The whole progress of the soul consists in its being moved by God", all our prayer is the prayer of the Holy Spirit within us, but it is still *our* prayer, the loving reticence of the Holy Ghost does not allow him to swamp or absorb our personal part and response, which is "placing ourselves in a state to receive this motion". Ascetical theology is but the experience of the Church as to how best this response can be achieved, it is the science of co-operation with the Holy Spirit. There is no sounder truth than that "after all, we must fall back on the grace of the Holy Spirit", and it must never be forgotten. But I must confess that I find nothing so infuriating as writers or directors who express this truism at the conclusion of every other sentence, and I do not think there is anything impious in accepting the axiom once and for all.

Finally, just to make everything gloriously impossible, it must be admitted that if God is not bound to his own ordinances, then neither is the Holy Ghost bound to ascetical theology! But I think, in both cases, we are. The Church is still enriched by those few chosen souls—quite "ordinary" souls—whose influential lives seem to soar towards sanctity while breaking all the rules there are—including the principle of Rule! These are those favoured ones of—there is no other phrase—unorthodox orthodoxy. If the reader belongs to this small group, he may burn this book and all like it, but curiously he probably will do nothing of the kind. Meanwhile, for the rest of us, serious training and slow struggle, not brilliance but stamina, is God's chosen way.

GLOSSARY

THE FOLLOWING short Glossary is compiled for the sole purpose of helping the ordinary Christian to understand the general trend of books on prayer. A great many technical terms of theology and ascetic are very subtle and complicated; for example, NESTORIANISM is the subject of many lengthy books and no short definition can hope to teach very much about it. But if this term is completely new to a reader, I hope my definition will prove sufficient to give sense to any passage in which it occurs.

I have also included words in common use, which have a slightly different semi-technical meaning; like RULE, CHARITY, and SIMPLE. I have been content here, merely to try to point out the differences of use.

I hope that I have been nowhere positively inaccurate or misleading, but it is plain that any sort of scholarly composition would be a book in itself. I have merely tried to give the gist of meaning to the commoner words for the purpose explained in the Preface.

ABANDONMENT (to the divine Providence). A system of prayer associated with M. Bousset: Cf. INDIFFERENCE of St Ignatius Loyola. Surrender to the will of God, prayer of quiet, cultivation of the "Peace of God", detachment from worldly ambition.

ACT (of prayer). Usually a set form of words with emphasis on the will; ACT of faith; a volitional prayer accompanied by effort of faith. ACTIVE life, ACTIVE (monastic order); that which includes practical works of charity, etc., as distinct from (pure) Contemplative life.

ACTUAL (sin, recollection, grace, etc.). Acts of these as opposed to "original" sin or HABITUAL grace, recollection; isolated acts against continuous habits in spiritual life.

ACQUIRED (grace, virtue, etc.). That gained partially by personal struggle, opposite to INFUSED; that which is a free and unsought gift of God.

ADORATION. The highest form of all prayer; the creature's response to God alone irrespective of his gifts, wholly objective worship, perfect self-giving to God. The only possible response to the BEATIFIC VISION. (*See* p. 106.)

AFFECTIVE (prayer). That in which our love for God is manifest, usually accompanied by a certain emotion and feeling. Generally accepted as the second stage in the spiritual life, one higher than meditation or prayer by mere duty.

ANGER. One of the Capital sins. Inordinate desire for revenge; psychological root of violence.

ANTHROPOMORPHISM. The crude application of human qualities to God; seeing God in human terms; as Genesis 2.2, "God rested on the seventh day", 3.8, "God walked in the garden in the cool of the day".

ANTINOMIAN, -ISM. One who rejects, the rejection of; all law. The theory that if we try to love God we are under no other obligation at all: that Grace liberates from all moral obligation.

APOCALYPTIC. Direct, mystical, relevation of divine truth; often presented in allegorical language; as the APOCALYPSE of St John, the Book of Revelation.

APOLLINARIANISM. The heresy that tends to deny the true Humanity of Christ.

APOLOGETIC. The establishment of Christian doctrine by reason, the intellectual defence of the Faith; not quite the same as "apology".

ARIDITY. Periods of "dryness", "staleness", apathy, or dullness for spiritual things. A very common experience in the life of prayer, when everything seems to go wrong (pp. 129–32).

ARIANISM. The heresy that tends to deny the true Divinity of Christ. Cf. APOLLINARIANISM.

ASCETIC. The doctrine of prayer, the branch of theology dealing with the spiritual life. Often misunderstood to mean mere austerity or exaggerated self-discipline of "Puritan" implication, as in ASCETICISM. Literally the "athletic training" of the spiritual athlete. Elementary and "acquired" exercises in prayer as opposed to MYSTICISM, which is largely infused and rare. The study of human progress towards perfection.

ASPIRATION. Acts of will in prayer, similar to an (ejaculatory) "act" of prayer. Volitionally to ASPIRE to the love of God.

ATTACHMENT (to creatures, people, etc.). Inordinate affection for worldly things; interest in, love for, things other than God, that hinders the spiritual life.

Attrait. French; "attraction", types of prayer, Rule, etc., attractive to a particular soul: the innate predisposition of a person to a particular kind of spirituality.

Attrition. Imperfect Contrition, sorrow for sin for some lower motive than the love of God, as fear of worldly consequences, punishment, etc.

Baptism. Sacrament whereby the soul is incorporated into the glorified Humanity of Christ; that which "makes a Christian" (pp. 8–13).

Beatific Vision. Perfectly to see God as he is in himself. The ultimate state of human blessedness, the experience of the perfected saints in heaven.

Beginners. Souls in the "Purgative Way". Serious, sincere, and possibly quite gifted Christians who have not reached spiritual stability or maturity (Proficients). Terms common to ascetic, but which may slightly change their meaning according to age and context. (*See* Preface.)

Belief. Largely intellectual acceptance of propositions, acceptance of Creeds, etc., by reason. Thus different from Faith, which is concerned with activity and will.

Benedictine. Pertaining to St Benedict of Nursia, founder of the Benedictine Order and Rule.

Betrothal (Spiritual). A common analogy in ascetical writings; the "marriage" of the soul with God; the Church, or individual Christians, as "spouse" or "bride" of Christ.

Besetting Sin. The main temperamental or personal temptation, or sin, that besets a particular soul. The sin a person most frequently commits, or finds most difficult to avoid.

Calvin, -ism. Pertaining to John Calvin, intellectual founder of modern Protestantism. In general inclined to Puritanism, anti-sacramental, anti-priestly; emphasis on doctrine of Predestination.

Capital Sins. (*See*) *Pride, Envy, Anger, Covetousness, Sloth, Lust, Gluttony*. The Root sins of both theology and psychology, and the most advanced and exhaustive system of self-examination. Commonly mis-called the Seven "Deadly" sins.

Cardinal Virtues. (*See*) *Justice, Temperance, Fortitude, Prudence.*

Carmelite. Monastic Order and school of spirituality, particularly sixteenth- and seventeenth-century Spanish: St Teresa of Avila, St John of the Cross. Ascetical system of great elaboration.

CARTHUSIAN. Monastic Order and school of spirituality.

CASUISTRY. The application of universal principles to particular cases, especially in moral theology. An essential part of Christian ethics, misused in derogatory sense (p. 160).

CATHOLIC. Almost impossible to define fairly because of sin, schism, and prejudice. But CATHOLIC CHURCH; the glorified Humanity of Christ into which souls are incorporated by Baptism, the "Body of Christ" on earth (MILITANT) in paradise (EXPECTANT) and in heaven (TRIUMPHANT). CATHOLIC THEOLOGY is doctrine which is "orthodox", embedded in history from the first century onwards; that of continuous historical tradition. Against "Protestantism" by emphasis on Sacramental mediation between soul and God, Supernaturalism, and Church as organic rather than individualistic.

CHALCEDONIAN DEFINITION. The orthodox statement of the relation between the two natures in the Person of Christ; similar to latter part of the "Athanasian Creed" in B.C.P. From Council of Chalcedon 451.

CHARITY. Greatest of the "theological virtues" (1 Cor. 13). The love of God for Creation and man's response to it. Selfless love for Our Lord alone, and for others in and through him. Tragically misused and abused in popular use.

CHASTITY. One of the "evangelical counsels". The right use of the sexual instinct either in marriage or celibacy—with which it is not to be confused. Nor to be confused with the suppression of this instinct.

CHRISTO-CENTRIC. Religion centred upon the second Person of the Holy Trinity to the exclusion of the other Persons; usually a rather sentimental attitude to Jesus.

CHRISTOLOGY. Theology relating to the two natures in the One Person of Christ; e.g. the Chalcedonian Definition.

CISTERCIAN. Monastic Order and school of spirituality, associated especially with St Bernard of Clairvaux: emphasis on the humanity of Christ, hence anti-Apollinarian.

COLLOQUY. Private prayer in the form of a personal conversation between the soul and God; what is usually meant by "saying your prayers", but not quite the same as "vocal prayer" (pp. 87ff.).

COMPOSITION OF PLACE. The initial use of the imagination in mental prayer. Imagining or picturing the scene of the narrative on which one is about to meditate.

CONATION. Psychological term: the innate, human urge to action; the undeveloped "will". The seat of human endeavour. Thence Spinoza calls the "soul" or inner principle of the human being "CONATUS".

CONCUPISCENCE. Vehement desire for the things of this world, including but not confined to, sexual passion; similar to, and rather stronger than, "attachment"; innate moral disorder.

CONSCIENCE. Instinctive human moral principle; moral consciousness needing training and direction, and never infallible—as taught by some non-Catholic ethicists.

CONSOLATION. A wide ascetical term embracing any kind of pleasant experience in prayer, particularly the vivid and consoling sense of God's Presence.

CONTEMPLATION. A "high" or "advanced" form of prayer which is not vocal or discursive; prayer which contains no words or thoughts; a "mystical" association with God; an illumination of the soul by God. But often used very ambiguously by ascetical writers—a difficult word.

CONTRITION. True Christian penitence; sorrow for sin based only on the love of God, without personal motive or fear.

CONVERSION. An infused act of God on the will, initiating the Christian life and leading to Baptism.

COUNSEL. 1. Intuitive, or "infused" wisdom; one of the "gifts of the Spirit". "Sanctified common sense." 2. Professional and technical guidance based on an objective body of doctrine. Quite different from general "advice" of a personal nature (pp. 42–3). 3. The Evangelical COUNSELS; *Poverty*, *Chastity*, and *Obedience*; Ordinances of Christ applicable to all Christian life by adaptation—not confined to the Monastic life.

COVETOUSNESS. One of the Capital sins: inordinate love of wealth, greed for material possessions, inordinate ambition leading to this; miserliness, inordinate "attachment to creatures".

CREATURE. Anything created, any part of the Creation, everything other than God. Slightly different from common use.

DARKNESS, DARK NIGHT OF THE SOUL. An "advanced" stage in the spiritual life, when personality becomes deadened to the world and to its senses and feelings in order to be illuminated by God in Contemplation. A kind of extreme and continuous aridity; the term is especially associated with the teaching of St John of the Cross.

DEISM. The theory that there is no, or little, relation between the world and God; belief in the existence of God but not in revelation. "Natural" not "revealed" religion, extreme transcendentalism.

DEPRAVITY, TOTAL. Protestant doctrine that the fallen human soul is wholly and utterly corrupt.

DESOLATION. Aridity, the feeling of being forsaken by God, the opposite term to "Consolation".

DESPAIR. The sin of giving up hope. Similar to ordinary use, but frequently found in ascetical writing to denote faithlessness caused by aridity or sin.

DETACHMENT. The opposite of "Attachment". Temperance in use of, or interest in, creatures. Freedom from worldly desires and interests.

DETERMINISM. Rejection of human freewill, fatalism, idea that all events are pre-determined by God or some other power; attitude of "what will be, will be". Thus ineffectiveness of prayer.

DEVOTIO MODERNA. School of spirituality emphasizing prayer of laity opposed to monasticism in fifteenth century. Includes the popular devotional work "On the Imitation of Christ" attributed to Thomas à Kempis.

DIFFIDENCE. Semi-technical term, similar to common use; fear of bad prayer, tension, scrupulosity; fear of dangers encountered in prayer.

DIRECTION. Help and guidance in prayer of one soul by another, application of ascetical theology to needs of the individual soul. (*See* Chapter 4.)

DISCERNMENT OF SPIRITS. Ascetical directions, rules or system, for examining the reality or value of "feelings" in prayer; a method of judgement regarding the meaning of religious experiences.

DISCURSIVE (PRAYER). Mental prayer consisting of a disciplined chain of thought; logical reasoning in prayer as opposed to Affective or Contemplative prayer. The ordinary process of normal meditation.

DISTRACTIONS. Mind wandering in prayer, that which hinders concentration in mental or vocal prayer; idle thoughts, feelings, or outside noises, etc., which hinder prayer.

DRYNESS. Common term for ARIDITY.

EBIONITES. Early heretics who wished to combine Christianity with Judaism, and make some of the Jewish "Law" binding on Christians. Still found in Sabbatarianism, etc.

Ego-centric. Self-centred, subjective, opposite to Theo-centric.

Ejaculation. A very short prayer of recollection using words, e.g. "Lord have mercy", "O God", or even just "Jesus". Usually of volitional and emotional content. Similar to Aspiration.

Election, The. Part of the *Spiritual Exercises* of St Ignatius Loyola; a systematic method of prayer applied to the making of important personal decisions. Election is sometimes used for the doctrine of Predestination.

Empirical. Of prayer and direction, experimental against formal or dogmatic; development of personal prayer by mutual discussion and experiment not authoritative order.

English School. Very important school of spirituality, especially in fourteenth-century and Caroline periods; but of continuous tradition from twelfth-century to today. Anglicans please note!

Envy. One of the Capital sins; sadness or jealousy at the good of another; ambition that envies another's position, promotion or success. Jealousy at other's personal qualities, dissatisfaction with one's own gifts and accomplishments. Envy applies to personal qualities as Covetousness applies to material goods.

Epistemology. The science of truth; philosophical examination of the grounds of knowledge.

Erastianism. The theory that the Church is subservient to, or a department of, the State.

Eremetical. Pertaining to hermits, those who seek God alone as opposed to Monastics which seeks God in communities. Particularly applied to the Fathers of the Egyptian desert.

Error, (also Ignorance) note ascetical distinction: *Vincible* error, that which can and should be overcome, implying a certain duty of pursuit of knowledge—the principle that "ignorance is no excuse". And *invincible* error or ignorance; that which is excusable.

Eschatology. The theology of the "Four Last Things"; *Death, Judgement, Heaven,* and *Hell*. Doctrines relating to the end of the world.

Eternal. A difficult word, "outside" time, ontological; *not* "everlasting".

Eudaemonism. Moral system based on the pursuit of happiness (hedonism) thus in ascetic, the inordinate desire for consolation in prayer and subjective pleasure in worship or religion;

the idea that the sole or main purpose of religion is to "make you feel happy".

EUTYCHES, -IANISM (or "psycho-physical-parallelism"). The heresy that says Christ has only one Nature, a mixture of human and divine, therefore strictly neither. In mental prayer, failure to see Christ as both perfectly God and perfectly Man.

EXERCISES, SPIRITUAL. Acts of imagination, intellect and will, as a preparation for prayer; mental prayer; acts conducive to prayer. *The* Spiritual Exercises usually means the system of St Ignatius Loyola.

FAITH. Volitional, rather than intellectual, acts; the dynamic of religion, the spur to activity in life and religion. cf. BELIEF.

FACULTY. One of the powers of the soul, imagination, memory, will, etc., used by medieval writers in a way tending to "split up" personality, hence "faculty psychology".

FASTING as religious discipline, closely related to recollection. A generally stronger term than abstinence, but ambiguous.

FAULT. A breach of Rule for whatever motive, therefore an amoral term, not to be confused with "sin" in any sense, pp. 50–1.

FORMALISM. Excessive adherence to prescribed forms. In ascetic, the exaggeration of liturgical Offices, etc., to the exclusion of private prayer and personal religion; adherence to the letter rather than the spirit of Rule, tendency to put bare duty before quest for progress.

FORTITUDE. One of the Cardinal virtues. In ascetic especially, spiritual stamina, a refusal to be discouraged by aridity, seeming lack of progress and consolations, or religious excitement. A characteristic of spiritual maturity.

FRANCISCAN. Pertaining to St Francis of Assisi, Order of Friars Minor, school of spirituality. cf. SALESIAN.

GENERAL CONFESSION. 1. The corporate form of confession in the Mass. 2. Personal confession in sacrament of Penance covering the whole life, as distinct from *particular* Confession covering only the period since the last previous confession.

GERMAN SCHOOL. School of spirituality flourishing mainly in thirteenth and fourteenth centuries; notable for Eckhart, Tauler, Suso, Ruysbroek, etc.

GIFTS, SPIRITUAL. 1. Particular attributes given to unique souls by God, see 1 Cor. 12, but also 2. GIFTS OF THE SPIRIT, a traditional ascetic classification; *Holy Fear, Godliness, Wisdom, Understanding, Knowledge, Counsel, Ghostly Strength.*

Glory. The state of God himself, the final blessedness of human sanctity; Christ Glorified, as he now is "on the right hand of the Father"; transfigured, ascended.

Gluttony. One of the Capital sins; excessive indulgence in *all* bodily appetites, food, drink, drugs, sex (cf. Lust), comfort, pleasure, etc., including "fussiness" as well as greed.

Gnosticism. System claiming advanced, occult, knowledge of spiritual things; often fantastic and arising from false mysticism. Cf. Agnostic, a sceptic about the faith, one who "does not know".

Grace. A difficult word to define; the action of God upon, or in, the depths of the soul. Qualified by "actual" and "habitual", also "Sacramental", "sanctifying", "prevenient", etc.

Guide. Term sometimes used for "Director" (of souls).

Habitual. Common ascetical term qualifying "Grace", "Sin", "Recollection", etc. That which is continuous, or forming a regular habit, distinct from "actual".

Holiness. Literally and correctly "wholeness", completeness, hence "perfection". Opposite to "partial" or dismembered rather than to "wicked".

Hope. One of the Theological Virtues. That which fixes the soul on God and drives it towards its true end. Faith in the knowledge and Providence of God.

Humanism. Faith in human reason and morality without divine Grace. Non-supernatural, rejection of revealed religion, sacraments, etc., Pelagianism in extreme form. Faith in man to work out his own salvation. But a very wide term.

Humility. Knowledge of the soul's utter dependence on God; the virtue based on the knowledge that all good, value, and beauty is derived from God.

Idealism. Philosophical theory tending to deny the existence of matter; the only "real" things are "ideas"; the world only exists in the mind of the beholder: hence an ascetical relation with Manichaeism, Puritanism, Apollinarianism, etc., and all views opposed to the "sacramental" outlook.

Ignatian. Pertaining to the teaching of St Ignatius Loyola.

Ignorance. *See* Error.

Illumination. Intensive activity by God upon the cleansed soul, the soul enlightened by the inspiration of the in-dwelling Spirit; hence the Illuminative Way, the second of the classical "Three Ways", wherein God acts upon the soul purged from gross sin. The experience of PROPHETS.

IMAGINATION. A reputable attribute of the soul, the source of ideas and knowledge; commonly misunderstood to imply falsehood (pp. 72–3).

IMMANENT, -CE. The indwelling of God in the world or the soul, the closeness of God to the creation, the nearness of the Presence of God: hence IMMANENTAL prayer or religion; that which tends to exaggerate this aspect, becoming subjective, worldly or sentimental. Opposite to Transcendent.

IMMEDIATE. 1. That which is not mediated by a third party, the direct relation or action of God on the soul, without the mediation of priest, Church or sacrament: mystical, infused, also 2. IMMEDIATE PREPARATION (for Mass, Meditation, etc.) spiritual exercises or prayers just before, "immediately" before, as against "remote" or "proximate" preparation.

INFUSED. Qualifying Grace, Contemplation, etc., that which is given direct by God, and not "acquired" by human act or struggle.

INSPIRATION. Literally "inbreathing" of Holy Spirit, action of the Spirit on the soul, but usually less intense and spectacular in results than "Illumination".

INTERCESSION. Prayer, private or corporate, offered to God on behalf of another, especially for some definite need or blessing.

INTERIOR PRAYER. Term used by most ascetical Saints in all kinds of different ways; "spiritual" life, contemplation, affective prayer, prayer centred on the Holy Spirit in the soul. But it might mean anything!

INVOCATION (often "of Saints"). Calling upon Saints or others to act as intercessors for us. Asking for prayer on behalf of oneself or others.

JESUIT. Commonly a member of the Society of Jesus, but also type of spirituality developed from St Ignatius Loyola; a form of "modernized 'Ignatian'".

JESUS PRAYER. A form, or system, of Meditation or Recollection, emanating from the Eastern Orthodox Church.

JUSTIFICATION BY FAITH. The Doctrine of St Paul (Galatians, Romans) implying the superiority of Faith in Christ over the "works of the law". Anti-Pelagian doctrine, but exaggerated by some Protestant schools to reduce, or exclude, the value of devotion, prayer, sacraments, and acts of charity.

Justice. One of the Cardinal virtues. The God-given love of Truth and right; hence the inspirer of worship as that which is justly and rightly due to God. Also recognition of the rights of other men and things.

Last Things, the Four. See Eschatology.

Legalism. Excessive respect for the "letter of the law", Pharisaism, the misinterpretation of ascetical Rule, as a value in itself divorced from the growth of the soul. Insistence on duty against love.

Letters of Direction. A specific body of ascetical literature consisting of correspondence from a Director to his spiritual children. Particular, personal, ascetical guidance, carried out by the written word not orally.

Little Flower. A popular pseudonym for St Thérèse of Lisieux.

Liguorian. Method of meditation taught by St Alphonsus di Liguori.

Logos. Greek for the pre-existent Word, or second Person of the Holy Trinity; as in John 1.1–14. The eternal Son of God.

Loving Regard, Prayer of. An affective, or contemplative form of prayer, taught by St Teresa of Avila, and others; a simple look at Christ without words or discursive thoughts.

Lust. One of the Capital sins. Misuse of the sex instinct; this rather than its over-indulgence, which is gluttony.

Manichaeism. Heresy teaching that matter, and particularly the functions of the human body, is intrinsically evil; thus Puritanism, and extreme "asceticism".

Marriage, Spiritual. Similar to spiritual Betrothal, a common analogy or allegory in ascetical writing; the union of the soul with God. Probably inspired originally by the Song of Songs.

Meditation. Discursive spiritual exercise; usually but not necessarily, based on the "three-point" type, i.e. use of Imagination, Intellect and Will: a rather narrower term than Mental Prayer.

Memory. The psychological seat of imagination; important to ascetic in linking prayer with "sense-experience".

Mental Prayer. Any spiritual exercise leading to greater knowledge of God; prayer with the mind rather than with words. Thus a more comprehensive term than Meditation.

Method. A detailed system of mental prayer, usually associated with one of the Saints or schools of prayer (Franciscan, Oratorian Method, etc.) and often very complex.

MIXED LIFE. Life composed of both charitable works and Contemplation; similar to ACTIVE life; the normal Christian ideal.

MODALISM. Group of heresies (e.g. *Sabellianism*) tending to deny the full doctrine of the Trinity; by teaching that Father, Son, and Holy Ghost, are but modes or aspects of the One God, not distinct Persons.

MODERNISM. The application of "modern" knowledge, especially epistemology, psychology, and philosophy, to Christian doctrine. A complicated movement of usually but not necessarily, Protestant leaning.

MONACHISM. Another word for Monasticism.

MONARCHIAN. Another "modalist" heresy, akin to "Unitarianism".

MONASTIC, -ISM. The stable religious life in common; not to be confused with the life of the HERMIT or RECLUSE (a miser living alone, is often described as a "monastic" existence which is quite the opposite of the truth!). Monastic Orders are not to be confused with Mendicant Orders, which are less stable and were originally a revolt against Monasticism. "Monks" are not to be confused with "friars". But it is a very wide and comprehensive term, embracing many Orders of great divergence.

MONOTHEISM. The doctrine that there is only one God.

MORALISM. "Practical", non-spiritual, ethical system; morality divorced from religion.

MORAL THEOLOGY. Systematic doctrine of Christian ethics; not to be confused with any other system—especially not with today's conventional view-point.

MORTAL SIN. That which "breaks" the relation of the soul with God, as against VENIAL SIN which "strains" the relation. Sin committed on purpose, with full knowledge, and of serious nature. A useful distinction if not too rigidly applied.

MORTIFICATION. Bodily discipline for spiritual purposes; self-denial, or self-restraint, as an aid to prayer.

MYSTICISM. An immediate, or direct, relation between the soul and God; spiritual experience transcending thought or logical reason; prayer independent of the senses.

NATURE. The state of NATURE often means unredeemed humanity, as opposed to the state of GRACE. The unbaptized, those not "in Christ". The State of "fallen" Creation.

NESTORIANISM. The heresy that divorces the two natures in the

Person of Christ one from the other. In ascetic the idea that Christ is God sometimes and Man at other times: that he is God at Mass on Sunday and Man at work on Monday!

NOSEGAY, SPIRITUAL. Fruits of meditation "gathered up" and taken out into life as recollection; looking back at the fruit of a previous meditation. Associated with the teaching of St François de Sales.

NOUMENAL. Intuitive, not known by the senses, therefore opposite to PHENOMENAL; associated especially with Kant.

NOVICIATE. A preparatory period of trial or experiment before embracing Rule, or taking monastic vows. A NOVICE is one making this test.

NUMINOUS. A common semi-mystical sense of the presence of God, the "atmosphere" of "holiness" in the arts or in nature; the religious "feeling" of a consecrated building. Used especially by Dr Rudolf Otto.

OBEDIENCE, HOLY. Obedience to dictates of the Church, or to the decisions of a religious superior, or director.

OBSCURANTISM. The principle of frustrating or preventing learning, especially that leading to new knowledge. Withholding certain doctrines from the laity. Common in modern ascetic in the idea of "simple religion", and the quest for devotion divorced from theology.

OBJECTIVE. Directed away from self, or TRUTH outside, and independent of, personal acceptance. OBJECTIVE PRAYER, or WORSHIP; that which is directed towards God rather than towards self or people; independent of personal feeling, emotion or interest.

OCCASIONS, OF SIN. Circumstances likely to lead a soul into sin; to an alcoholic, a pub could be an "occasion of sin". Bad books and films, evil company, etc., could be "occasions of sin". But it is a subjective term, "occasions of sin" depend on the soul concerned; and may be neither good nor bad in themselves.

OFFICE. The "official" daily worship of the Church, the objective, corporate prayer of the Church. The "Hours" of Prayer, or Anglican Matins and Evensong.

OMNIPOTENCE. The power, majesty, "almightiness" of God; all-powerful, infinite.

OMNIPRESENCE. Present at all times and in all places; God being "everywhere".

OMNISCIENCE. Infinite knowledge of God; that God "knows everything".

ONTOLOGICAL. Pertaining to the philosophy of "Being", OBJECTIVE knowledge, eternal, truth independent of the human world.

OPUS DEI. "The work of God", a term applied to the daily Office by St Benedict.

ORATORIAN usually refers to seventeenth-century French school of spirituality, including St John Eudes, M. Olier. It emphasizes the Adoration of the Father by the Son.

ORIGINAL SIN. The sin of Adam, thence the general sinfulness of the human race; the state of the soul before Baptism, the soul's sinfulness apart from its ACTUAL sin, i.e. sins "actually" committed. Sin shared in common, not "hereditary".

ORTHODOX. "Catholic" or traditional, as popular use; but as used to qualify "prayer", "spirituality", etc., it usually means pertaining to the Eastern Orthodox Church.

PANTHEISM. The theory that God *is* everything, thus that the world is God, or a part of him. Thus, in ascetic, nature-worship, etc.

PARADISE. The realm of the Church Expectant, the sphere of the faithful departed proceeding towards perfection. The word implies the blessedness of this state as nearer to God than those in the world, and without earthly limitation, but see also PURGATORY.

PARTICULAR. Confession or self-examination confined only to the period since the last previous occasion, as distinct from GENERAL confession, etc., dealing with the whole life-time.

PASSIVE, PASSIVITY. Essentially the doctrine that God takes the initiative in every good work; prayer wherein the soul waits on God to guide it, against ACTIVITY where the soul actively tries to co-operate with God. A quiet waiting for God to act, thence surrender to his act and will: thus PASSION, that which Christ accepted, that which was done to him.

PELAGIANISM. The most prevalent (and pernicious) of pastoral heresy; condemned in the fourth century, still going strong. The denial of the need for Grace, thence that man can save his own soul by his own works and efforts; moralism, humanism; the idea that the Christian Faith consists of "doing good" without the need for sacraments, grace, prayer, or divine inspiration. Ultimately fulfilled in the idea that "I've never done any harm, therefore God ought to be very pleased with me."

Penance. An act of mortification in sorrow for sin, a prayer of contrition or thanksgiving after absolution. Sacramental confession.

Penitence. Contrition, sorrow for sin as against the love of God.

Penitent. One who habitually uses the sacrament of Penance, i.e., who goes to Confession.

Perfection. The highest human state in this world, after Proficiency. Not necessarily "perfect" in the usual sense, thus writers speak of "higher" or "lower" degrees of Perfection.

Periodicity. The fact that the spiritual life of the soul fluctuates over the years; that, while advancing in general, it has its good and dull periods (pp. 132–4).

Petition. Colloquy mainly about one's own personal needs.

Phenomenal. Philosophical term meaning that which is experienced by the senses; differs from common use in that any sense experience, however slight and insignificant, is a Phenomena.

Pietism. Exaggeration of religious feelings and emotions against intellectual doctrine; a rather sentimental movement within Lutheranism; rather "precious" religiosity.

Polytheism. The theory that there are many "gods".

Postulant. One preparing for the Novitiate, one stage lower than a Novice, an earlier preparatory period.

Predestination. The theory that God elects or chooses certain souls. Double Predestination, the view that some are inevitably "saved" and others inevitably "damned" by the choice of God, and irrespective of their own merit; associated with St Augustine of Hippo and Calvin.

Prevenient, Prevenience. The fact that God acts before man, that God "makes the first move", as in St John "not that we loved him but that he first loved us", "You have not chosen me, but I have chosen you". Thus Prevenient Grace, that which God supplies without our knowledge or act.

Pride. First of the Capital sins, and root of all sin. The belief that we can exist or do good works without the grace of God. Putting self before God, excessive self-love. The sin of Satan, open rebellion against God. The essence of Pelagianism.

Probabilism. A tenet of casuistry whereby, in cases of sincere moral doubt, a soul can freely choose the most "probably right"—the "lesser of evils"—without actual sin. The accepted and common-sense method of dealing with honest moral alternatives.

PROFICIENT. A mature Christian, more advanced than a BEGINNER, yet far from PERFECTION; a sound "ordinary" Christian.

PROXIMATE PREPARATION. In mental prayer, preparatory exercise between "remote" and "immediate" preparation; made a short time before prayer begins.

PRUDENCE. One of the Cardinal virtues; the practical wisdom of Christ in the members of his Body.

PSYCHIC. Natural susceptibility to supernatural forces, natural rather than Christian, "mystical" experience; non-discursive insight into the supernatural.

PSYCHOLOGICAL. Literally the science of the soul; how the human mind and spirit functions; discursive, logical sequence of experience. Much misused in popular speech.

PURGATION. The expulsion of sinful habits and tendencies from the life of the soul; the (successful) fight against sin. Thus the PURGATIVE WAY, the first of the classical "Three Ways" wherein the soul tries to conquer gross sin to allow God's ILLUMINATION.

PURGATORY. The same as PARADISE but stressing the necessarily painful part of the progress towards perfection in The Church Expectant.

PURITANISM. Strictly the quest for "pure Spirit" divorced from bodily or material aspects; thus non-Sacramental, and tending towards MANICHAEISM; attribution of evil to all bodily appetites, thus suspicion of pleasure or happiness.

PURITY. Nearly the exact reverse of Puritanism! essentially SINGLENESS of purpose in service of God by the whole personality. Holiness in the sense of wholeness, completeness, perfection of intention regarding God.

QUIET, PRAYER OF. Passive prayer, a simple "waiting upon God"; the disciplined use of Silence in a quiet search for God.

QUIETISM. Very different from Prayer of Quiet. The exaggeration of Passivity into the virtual annihilation of the power of the soul, as taught by Molinos. The denial of any kind of activity or co-operation with God in prayer.

RECIDIVIST. One who frequently falls into the same sins.

RECOLLECTION. 1. The state in which the soul is simple and unified, directing all its energies towards God; God-centred harmony. 2. Short acts of prayer, or the remembering of the divine Presence periodically; the "practice of the Presence of God". (*See* Chapter 6.)

REDEMPTION. Atonement, the cleansing from sin leading to ultimate glory; restoration of fallen nature by grace.

RELAPSING SINNER. One who has contracted a habit of sin. Cf. RECIDIVIST.

RELIGIOUS. Another name for a monk or nun: the RELIGIOUS LIFE usually means MONASTICISM.

REMOTE PREPARATION. Actual or habitual Recollection; general preparation for meditation made some hours before the actual time of prayer; consideration of next morning's prayer on retiring.

REPARATION. The attempt to make good damage done to another soul by sin, often following the Sacrament of Penance.

REPENTANCE. *See* PENITENCE, but possibly of slightly wider meaning, sometimes implying a mixture of Contrition and Attrition.

RESOLUTION. An act of will to do something definite for God; often the fruit of meditation.

RETREAT. A period of a few days spent in prayer and silence, sometimes with instruction and direction (pp. 125–7).

RIGHTEOUSNESS. Strictly, communion with God; the state of grace, much more than "goodness".

RULE. A single, systematic pattern of prayer and worship; a (personal) ascetical programme; a balanced composition of spiritual exercises. (*See* Chapter 5.)

SABELLIANISM. A "modal" heresy teaching that God the Father became Incarnate in Christ.

SACRAMENTAL. Pertaining to the Seven Sacraments of the Church; but frequently used in the wider sense of anything spiritual expressed by material means, e.g. the Arts, human relations, etc. Opinion is divided as to whether this is a legitimate use of the word.

SALESIAN. Pertaining to the teaching of St François (Francis) de Sales; note that "Franciscan" applies to St Francis of Assisi.

SCHOLASTIC. The teaching of the "Schoolmen" of the Middle Ages; the main stream of Christian philosophy and theology in the Middle Ages, especially St Thomas Aquinas.

SCRUPLES, SCRUPULOSITY. Spiritual or moral anxiety about little things; excessive worry about one's moral state; fear and morbidity in prayer.

SELF-EXAMINATION. A systematic consideration of personal sins, usually prior to Confession; a period of prayer for this purpose.

SENSIBLE (DEVOTION). Pertaining to the physical SENSES; prayer with feeling, the consolation of seeming to hear or see Christ. It does not mean "sane" or "intelligent" as in popular use.

SIMPLE, SIMPLICITY. Of the soul, unified, recollected, integrated; not distracted by self-will or unruly passion. Almost the opposite of popular use; thus a "simple soul" is usually one in a very advanced state.

SIN. An act contrary to the will of God; that which impedes spiritual progress; that which spoils or breaks the soul's relation with God. A term of moral theology much misused in popular speech.

SLOTH. One of the Capital sins, laziness in the pursuit of virtue, or in the exercise of prayer.

SOTERIOLOGY. Pertaining to the soul's salvation; generally exaggerated in Protestantism; a lower ideal than Adoration or sanctification.

SOUL. The whole integrated human personality, including mind and body; not to be confused with the "spirit" or "conatus".

SPACIAL. Occupying or existing in, space; thus NON-SPATIAL means outside worldly experience; spiritual or heavenly.

SPIRITUAL EXERCISES. *See* EXERCISES.

SUBJECTIVE. With emphasis on self; prayer which is centred on the soul rather than "objectively" on God; prayer with feeling and consolation, "interior" prayer.

SULPICIAN. School of spirituality, best known for a form of meditation (the SULPICIAN METHOD) based on the thought of Jesus "before the eyes", "in the heart", "in the hands".

SUPPLICATION. A composite word for most of the ordinary divisions of Colloquy.

SURRENDER. Similar to ABANDONMENT, but generally more of an "act" of prayer and less of a "method".

TEMPERANCE. One of the Cardinal virtues; closely related to "ascetic" as analogous to "athletic training" for prayer; nothing to do with teetotalism!

TEMPERAMENT. Characteristic make-up of personality; in ascetic, usually roughly classified as 1. *Melancholic*; serious, subjective, often scrupulous. 2. *Choleric*; self-assertive, arrogant, forceful. 3. *Sanguine*; easy-going, optimistic. 4. *Phlegmatic*; apathetic, dull, unemotional.

TEMPORAL. Of time as opposed to Eternity, a characteristic of this life.

TELEOLOGY. The view that all is moving to a purposeful end, or consummation directed by God; the faith that "God is working his purpose out".

THEISM. The philosophy that there is a relation between God and the world; widely sacramental. Christianity is THEISTIC.

THEO-CENTRIC. Centred on God; life, system, or prayer with God, not self or the world, as basis.

THEOLOGICAL VIRTUES. Ascetical and moral classification: *Faith, Hope, Charity.*

THOMISM. Pertaining to the teaching of St Thomas Aquinas.

TRACTARIAN. Nineteenth-century thought concerned with Anglo-Catholic Revival; the theology of the Oxford Movement; Keble, Pusey, etc. Often implying "early" Anglo-Catholicism.

TRANSCENDENCE. The fact that God is omnipotent, over, away from, apart from, independent of; the world. The opposite and complementary characteristic to IMMANENCE.

UNITIVE WAY. The last of the "Three Ways"; the state of general and continuous union with God.

VENIAL SIN. Sin not "mortal", less serious, that which "strains" but does not break off the soul's relation with God.

VICTORINE. School of spirituality in twelfth century; St Richard and St Hugh, of St Victor.

VOCAL PRAYER. A wide term for any sort of prayer in which words are used; may include Office or "set prayers". Cf. COLLOQUY.

VOLITION. The action of the will, pertaining to the will.

WAYS, THE THREE. Classical scheme of the progressive life of prayer; the *purgative* way, *illuminative* way, *unitive* way.

WORD (OF GOD). Ambiguous, since it can mean the literal spoken word, or teaching, of God, as in the Scriptures. But usually the *Logos*, or eternal Second Person of the Trinity; The Son of God as in John 1.1–14.

WORLD. Either the Creation, which is good if fallen; or the sinful attractions of natural life, which are bad. It is all very confusing!

SELECT BIBLIOGRAPHY

I HAVE TRIED to choose this short selection of books both for their *general* interest and for their relevance to the theme of this book. I stress *general* because, as I have pointed out in Chapter 4, a soul's *particular* requirement is properly a matter for personal guidance. For similar reasons I have left out "devotional" literature, both ancient and modern, as well as spiritual classics of the Saints: my own particular favourites may not inspire others and any attempt at an exhaustive list would run into many pages and mean little to an individual reader.

Of the great standard works of reference, the four listed are, I think, the most easily understood and rather better arranged and indexed than others; but these of course are hardly meant to be read for excitement or amusement! On the other hand I am sure it is a mistake to regard such works as the scholar's private preserve; used occasionally and sensibly they can be of far greater value to the layman than many a "popular" little book.

I Standard Works of Reference

Directorium Asceticum (English translation in four volumes). J. B. Scaramelli

Holy Wisdom. Fr Augustine Baker

The Elements of the Spiritual Life. F. P. Harton

The Theology of the Spiritual Life. Joseph de Guibert

II Pastoral Theology

Christ, the Christian and the Church. E. L. Mascall

Pilgrim's Programme. William Purcell

A Two-Way Religion. V. A. Demant

A Short Introduction to Moral Theology. Lindsay Dewar

The Christian Mysteries. Bede Frost

The Gospel in Slow Motion. R. A. Knox

Confession from Priest and Penitent. John C. Heenan

III Prayer: Instruction and Methods

The Art of Mental Prayer. Bede Frost
Meditation and Mental Prayer. Wilfred L. Knox
Mental Prayer according to St Thomas Aquinas. D. Fahey
Practical Mysticism for Normal People. Evelyn Underhill
Concerning the Inner Life. Evelyn Underhill
Retreat to Advance. M. Carpenter-Garnier
A Retreat for Lay-folk. R. A. Knox

IV The Christian in the World

Faith and Society. M. B. Reckitt
Liturgy and Society. A. G. Hebert
Christianity and This World. A. R. Vidler
Essays in Liberality. A. R. Vidler
Essays and Addresses. F. von Hugel
Letters to a Niece. F. von Hugel
The Letters of Evelyn Underhill. Evelyn Underhill
Worship and its Social Significance. The I.C.F. Conference, 1939
The Religious Prospect. V. A. Demant
This Vast Activity. Mary McCulloch

INDEX

(* *Words marked with an asterisk are also included in Glossary*)